ON CALL WITH

DOCTOR FINLAY

PETER HAINING

Peter Haining has written several books on
television subjects, most notably
Dr Who: A Celebration, *The Television Sherlock
Holmes*, and previously for Boxtree,
The Complete Maigret. Starting as a local and
Fleet Street journalist, Peter then moved into
publishing, becoming publishing director of
New English Library before he eventually
decided to concentrate on writing full time.
He lives in Boxford, Suffolk.

ON CALL WITH

DOCTOR FINLAY

PETER HAINING

B🌿XTREE

SCOTTISH TELEVISION ENTERPRISES

For
Peter, David, Ian
Jason and Annette,
and the pleasure of their
company on the Call.

First published in Great Britain in 1994 by Boxtree Limited

Text © Peter Haining/Scottish Television Enterprises 1994
Photographs © Scottish Television Enterprises 1994

(with the exception of the following pages: pp.7, 23 – BBC Television; p.10 – *The Times* ; p.12, 21, 25, 28, 32, 35, 81 – Hulton Deutsch; pp.14, 17, 18 – New English Library; pp.18, 50, 51 – Stirling and Trossachs Tourist Board; p.37 [top] – *Dundee Courier*; p.37 [bottom] – *Daily Mail*)

1 3 5 7 9 10 8 6 4 2

Designed by Anita Ruddell

Printed and bound in Italy by New Interlitho, Milan, for
Boxtree Limited
Broadwall House
21 Broadwall
London SE1 9PL

A CIP catalogue entry for this book is available from the British Library.

ISBN: 1 85283 471 4

Front and back cover photographs courtesy of Scottish Television Enterprises.

Frontispiece: *David Rintoul as Dr John Finlay.*

Contents

THE LEGEND OF THE
GOOD DOCTOR

*I*T WAS PROBABLY one of the most unexpected returns of a famous television character to the small screen. With the sights and sounds of the carnage of war all around a huge army hospital in Berlin in 1946, a weary and dispirited young doctor was seen up to his elbows in blood and gore as he fought unavailingly to save yet another casualty of the savagery of battle.

In this memorable sequence, Major John

Finlay – the idealistic young GP better known as Dr Finlay who had last been seen on television some twenty years ago peacefully at work in a small rural community in 1920s Scotland – returned to the nation's screens, and those viewers old enough to have seen his earlier cases found themselves looking at a man of a totally new era. Here was a doctor scarred by what he had been through during the Second World War and who, after his demob, would soon find himself back in a drab, Orwellian Britain sunk in the austerity of a hard-won victory where the best hope of providing good medicine for ordinary men, women and children lay in the idea of a National Health Service.

The opening few minutes of Scottish Television Enterprises' (STE) new series *Doctor Finlay* was certainly a startling concept to those viewers who remembered the BBC's *Dr Finlay's Casebook* during its run from 1962–1971. At the same time, it provided a spectacular introduction to those younger viewers discovering the Scottish GP for the very first time. For both groups, it marked a watershed in the enduring popularity of the television medical series.

The original *Dr Finlay's Casebook* is, of course, now a part of television folklore, and the news in 1992 that STE were planning to revive the leading characters immediately

(Opposite) *Major John Finlay prepares himself to leave the army hospital in Berlin and return to Tannochbrae.*

(Below) *The original cast of* Dr Finlay's Casebook *in a typical scene from the famous BBC series of the 1960s.*

sparked a widespread discussion in the media about nostalgia and the inevitability of comparisons being made between the two series. Indeed, the statements of the company's Controller of Drama, Robert Love, and Peter Wolfes, the producer of the new series, were almost drowned in this deluge of opinions. They are both worth restating, however, to put the intentions of the programme – which attracted audiences in excess of eleven million for the first six episodes, is now in its second series, and has a third already guaranteed – clearly into perspective.

Speaking in July 1992 when the project was announced, Robert Love said: 'We have updated the series without losing the essential ingredients, particularly the relationship between the central characters, which made the original so popular. Setting *Finlay* in the Forties also allows the writers to explore storylines such as the difficulties of post-war life and the changes that health care was undergoing at the time.'

To suggestions that the new series was an unabashed exercise in nostalgia, Love added: 'The mood that we're responding to is that people have possibly tired of gritty reality and would like something a bit softer, a bit warmer, and closer to home. Life is kind of harsh out there, and sometimes it's nice to see people on your screen that you like and can identify with and feel glad to welcome into your home.'

Peter Wolfes was even more specific on the subject of nostalgia. 'We acknowledge that the characters are based on AJ Cronin's, but that's where the similarity to the first series stops. This is not a remake. Not a recreation. I have not asked the actors to do impersonations. The classic *Finlay* was made in the 1960s and set in the 1920s: for the contemporary audience this was nostalgia, a time half-remembered and still talked about. But for today's viewers that period is history; we need to update it to the immediate post-war period to get the sense of a time just back down the road which our parents knew and talked about.'

Just how determined Peter Wolfes was to distance *Doctor Finlay* from its predecessor may be judged from his own admission that there was a long debate at STE about actually dropping the GP's name from the title and calling the series simply, *The Good Doctor*. Peter would have also preferred to rename the town of Tannochbrae, which he felt was 'a bit twee' for modern audiences.

What he has done, however, is to film the series entirely on location and use scenes from many different places, 'to give the programme a life outside just the central characters'. At the same time, he decided equally firmly *not* to film in Callander, the location of the original BBC series, which subsequently became a tourist attraction as a result of the association. The dismay of the people in the Perthshire town was matched by the joy of those in Auchtermuchty in Fife which Peter and his production team finally chose as their new Tannochbrae.

In casting the leading players, it was also decided that native-born Scots were essential – and although David Rintoul, Ian Bannen and Annette Crosbie were all familiar with the original series, each brought a new interpretation to their respective parts: Rintoul becoming a more worldly-wise and volatile Doctor Finlay, Bannen crusty and conniving as Dr Cameron, and Janet with a life of her own beyond Arden House and even a lover. The introduction of a new character, the abrasive young Dr Neil, also signalled that there was to be no reprise for some of the other old favourites from the *Casebook* like Dr Snoddie and Mistress Niven, now considered too folksy and whimsical for stories set in the post-war era.

David Rintoul as Dr Finlay, Ian Bannen as Dr Cameron, Annette Crosbie as Janet, and newcomer Dr Neil played by Jason Flemyng.

The revival of *Doctor Finlay* has naturally regenerated interest in its predecessor, which has been referred to in the history of TV as the 'first exercise in television nostalgia'. And although the fact was probably not appreciated at the time, *Dr Finlay's Casebook* changed the perception that many English viewers had about the Scots, as a nation dressed in kilts who were addicted to country dancing, into one of a kind and gentle people full of uncomplicated common sense.

Undeniable, too, is that the success of the *Casebook* – along with contemporaries such as *Maigret, Z-Cars,* and ITV's *The Power Game* and *The Avengers* – led television into a new era of competitive scheduling prompted by a public who demonstrated that they had a liking for the same engaging characters turning up in different stories each week.

The success of the new *Doctor Finlay* – which is now being shown in eight countries including America, New Zealand, Sweden, Denmark, Finland, Iceland, Slovenia and Croatia, with considerable interest also coming from a number of other European broadcasters as well as Australia – has already attracted its fair share of theories attempting to explain that appeal. A hankering for nostalgia, the perennial interest in the lives of doctors, and the morbid fascination with illness are just three that already come in for lively debate among television critics and feature writers. A leading psychologist at Glasgow University has even claimed that 'sex' is another reason for this success, according to a report in the *Evening News* of 2 April 1993. The psychologist (who, curiously, was not named) maintained that *Doctor Finlay* dealt with sex in a very subtle, but effective way. The paper then went on to quote him.

> *'The likes of Finlay can satisfy the sexual impulses of many women. What you have on TV is a man who deals with issues of personal crises on a safe level. Women can relate to him as a strong figure and he has a very acceptable way of touching on people's anxieties and problems. Many women find that very comforting.'*

ON CALL WITH DOCTOR FINLAY

Whatever the reasons for its popularity, *Doctor Finlay* has been generously praised by viewers and the media alike and has added yet another dimension to the legend which now surrounds the trio of characters brought to life in the fertile imagination of the Scottish writer who was himself a country GP before becoming a best-selling novelist. It is his story, as well as that of the two television series he inspired, which I have set out to tell in the pages that follow: a story which reveals some intriguing misconceptions and painful memories about the original *Dr Finlay's Casebook*, as well as the imagination, determination and dedication which has gone into the making of STE's *Doctor Finlay*.

It is an account not without its share of humour too, and of all these stories perhaps the most ironic concerns a tape of the first episode of the new series – copies of which were sent out for review, in the normal fashion, to all the Glasgow newspapers. One recipient was a reviewer from the *Daily Telegraph* who, after viewing the tape, dutifully sent it back.

Unfortunately, the poor man got the return address wrong and despatched the package to an address in Queen Margaret Drive in Glasgow instead of to STE's headquarters in Cowcaddens, also in Glasgow. The embarrassed reviewer later said he thought the series had been made by the BBC.

Cartoon of the new Doctor Finlay *from* The Times *(6 March 1993).*

Chapter Two

THE MAN WHO WAS
DOCTOR FINLAY

D O NOT IMAGINE that I was the admirable Crichton of Tannochbrae, a blameless young medic who was never stupid, fatuous or foolish. More than once I was all three.

At first glance these lines might easily be taken as a snatch of dialogue from any television production featuring Dr Finlay. In fact, they were written almost half a century ago by the doughty Scot who created the Good Doctor – and he was speaking about himself.

Many writers have been inspired to create their most enduring characters from their own experiences of people close to them. Sir Arthur Conan Doyle, for example, based Sherlock Holmes on Dr Thomas Bell, his tutor at Edinburgh University who was famous for his powers of observation, while Agatha Christie took her grandmother, a lady blessed with an uncanny insight into human nature, as the model for her redoubtable spinster detective Miss Marple.

AJ Cronin, however, *was* Dr Finlay – just as his own experiences as a young doctor in a small West Highland town were the inspiration for the stories and adaptations which have since made Finlay arguably the most famous country doctor on television. Yet, although the character of the resourceful and idealistic young GP is now firmly established in the public imagination, the man who created him remains something of an enigma more than a decade after his death. A naturally dour

and somewhat reclusive man, Cronin spent the closing years of his life in Switzerland, and although in his autobiography, *Adventures in Two Worlds,* published in 1952, he revealed some of the details of his life as a doctor, there was very little about the success that followed his string of best-selling novels and the international public acclaim for his character Dr Finlay on television.

I met Cronin in the late Sixties when I was the Editorial Director of New English Library, the London publishers of the paperback editions of his famous novels. I was also the editor responsible for the first publication of *Adventures of a Black Bag,* a collection of short stories about Dr Finlay, his colleagues and the people of Tannochbrae. It was, in fact, his first book to be solely devoted to Finlay. Cronin had written the stories originally for magazines and some had been utilized for the BBC TV series, *Dr Finlay's Casebook*, in 1962. Retrieving these colourful tales from the files for their first book publication in 1969, when the doctor was already a household name, was a satisfying experience – all the more so because the titles of some of the stories were so evocative of the TV series itself: 'The Man Who Came Back', 'Enter Nurse Angus', 'Who Laughs Last' and 'Finlay's Drastic Cure'.

I remember, in particular, coming across a paragraph in one of the stories, 'The Resolution That Went Wrong'. For in it,

(Opposite) AJ Cronin, the creator of Dr Finlay, studied and practised medicine until 1930 when he gave it up to devote himself to writing.

Cronin offered another revealing insight into the character of his doctor which seemed to me to go a long way towards explaining his universal appeal both in print and on the small screen:

'It would be pleasant to exhibit Finlay in the best Victorian tradition, a strong and silent youth whose glittering pledges were never unfulfilled. But Finlay was human. Finlay had as much to put up with as you or I. And, often as not, circumstances played spillikins with his most fervent resolutions.'

The paperback edition of these stories was released by New English Library (NEL) in May 1969 and became a bestseller. Then, almost ten years later, Bob Tanner, the Managing Director of NEL visited Cronin in his Swiss home and secured his agreement for a second collection, which appeared in 1978 as *Dr Finlay of Tannochbrae* and enjoyed similar success. Unlike its predecessor, this collection appeared in hardcovers and was illustrated with a number of evocative line drawings by David Dowland and Joyce Smith.

Cronin was certainly pleased by the success of *Dr Finlay* on television – although he did have to counsel the BBC against over-exposing the series, as I shall reveal in the next chapter. But he took even greater satisfaction from the public and critical acclaim of his other novels such as *Hatter's Castle* (1931), *The Stars Look Down* (1935), *The Citadel* (1937), *The Keys of the Kingdom* (1942), and *The Spanish Gardener* (1950), all of which were best-sellers and made into popular films. The financial security that these books brought him meant that he could live where he chose and write what he wanted. 'I was a wee bit taken aback when *Finlay* became such a success on television,' he admitted years later in his deep Scottish burr. 'I thought it might last for a while, but never all those years. Aach, the man struck a chord in folks.'

Cronin's last home on a sweep of hillside at Vevey in Switzerland was very unlike the simple Scottish croft where he had grown up. Imposing without being ostentatious, the house was filled with a fine collection of modern art which he bought with his literary earnings. One of his neighbours was Charlie Chaplin and the two men became good friends. Cronin, in fact, was always more willing to talk about the great film comedian than himself: 'Every year they had a carnival in Vevey,' he said in 1978, the year after Chaplin's death, 'and wee Charlie used to dress up in his tramp's outfit and lead the procession. Mind ye, he was always worrying about his health. He even had a small operating theatre built in his home in case he needed treatment.'

Cronin enjoyed several trips to Hollywood to see his books being filmed and, during one of these, became friendly with the legendary couple, Spencer Tracy and Katharine Hepburn. 'Gee, how I loved that gal,' he once said of the actress.

Throughout his life, the tall, distinguished-looking Cronin never lost his 'Scottishness' and in Switzerland would not let a day pass without tuning in his long-range radio to find out from the BBC what was happening in his native country. And as if to provide an ever-present reminder of his origins and profession which had helped provide his passport to wealth and fame, he was looked after by a quietly-spoken and extremely effi-

cient housekeeper named Jane – indeed, very like the famous Janet of Tannochbrae.

Cronin, who was known to his friends and associates as 'AJ' (and signed all his letters in green ink with these initials), was born Archibald Joseph Cronin on 19 July 1896, the son of Patrick and Jessie Cronin, at Cardross, Dunbartonshire (now part of Strathclyde). The chances of a comparatively comfortable upbringing were unfortunately shattered when Cronin's father died while he was still a child and his mother had a struggle to make ends meet. A family decision that he should study for either the church or medicine was settled by the boy himself, who opted for doctoring as 'the lesser of two evils', as he later remarked with a touch of the pawky humour that peppered his conversations. (He was, nonetheless, a devout Catholic.)

Through the sheer hard work that was to characterize his early years, Cronin won a Carnegie scholarship and went to Glasgow University. His studies were interrupted, however, by the outbreak of the First World War. Called into the Royal Naval Reserve, he ultimately became a Surgeon Sub-Lieutenant and thanks to study and the practical experience he gained from this work, he graduated with a MB, ChB with honours in 1919. He was then appointed physician to the outpatients department of Bellahouston War Pensions Hospital and afterwards Medical Superintendent at Lightburn Hospital, Glasgow, where he experienced some of the kind of incidents that were to prove invaluable when he later turned to writing novels. When he was still at the Glasgow asylum, for instance, he was

The original NEL paperback editions of Adventures of a Black Bag *and* Adventures in Two Worlds.

very nearly strangled by one of the inmates; and during a period serving as ship's doctor on a cruise to Calcutta, a sudden outbreak of smallpox threatened to kill off the entire complement of passengers and crew.

It was in 1921 that fate brought him to the West Highlands and the little town (to which he gave the fictitious name of Tannochbrae in his autobiography) and its people who were to play such a significant part in his life. Arriving there to begin practising, he described his first sight of the place in *Adventures in Two Worlds*:

'The village, as the spring came, lost all its bleakness. Wrapped in soft airs, the blue sky feathered by fleecy clouds, the cottage gardens filled with the scent of honeysuckle and the hum of bees, the hillsides alive with the bleating of lambs, Tannochbrae became a sweet and pleasant place.'

Influential though the setting was, it was nothing compared to that of the senior partner of the rural practice:

'He was a medium-sized, oldish man with a face beaten bright crimson by Scots weather and Scots whisky,' Cronin wrote. *'He stooped slightly, so that his head had a forward, belligerent thrust. He wore gaiters, cord breeches and a big, baggy tweed jacket of a nondescript, vaguely greenish colour, the side pockets stuffed to the bursting point with everything from an apple to a gum-elastic catheter. About him there hung invariably the odour of drugs, carbolic and strong tobacco.'*

This was, of course, the real-life Dr Cameron. And equally formidable on first acquaintance (and equally real) was the Doctor's house-keeper, Janet:

'She was a thin, elderly woman, dressed entirely in black. Her hair was tightly drawn, her person spotless, and in her bleak face was stamped authority, mingled with a certain grudging humanity. She had the look, indeed, of one tempted terribly to smile, who guards perpetually against a single sign of levity, lest it ruin her self-esteem.'

During his two years in the practice, the young Cronin came to realize that Dr Cameron was really a rather sentimental old man, but was quite unable to reveal this side

Ian Bannen brought his own unique interpretation to the part of Dr Cameron in Doctor Finlay.

of his nature for fear of it being taken as a sign of weakness. Janet, too, disguised her affection for the two doctors with an imperturbability motivated by a strong sense of propriety. The young man also came to appreciate the different characters of the patients they served, too – those who were grateful and those who constantly complained – as well as the formidable district nurse Mistress Niven and the patronizing local health officer, Dr Snoddie, forever fingering his gold-rimmed pince-nez.

It was the death of Dr Cameron as a result of over-work and lobar pneumonia that forced the young Dr Cronin to make the next important decision in his life: whether to stay in Tannochbrae as Janet and many of the patients wanted him to do, or to move on to pastures new. He was by now anxious to marry his long-time sweetheart, Mary Gibson, who lived near Glasgow, and knew he would need a larger practice to support them both.

He therefore decided that the time had come to leave Scotland. But Tannochbrae, Dr Cameron, Janet and all the others would never leave his memory – although it was to be many years before he committed them to paper and began the process of making Dr Finlay a household name.

In fact, after his marriage to Mary, Cronin exchanged one demanding job for another when he took up the position of medical officer in a small mining village in South Wales. Here he experienced at first hand the grim life of miners, and in 1925 was involved in the disaster at Ystfad Colliery in Pengelly. As a result of an underground water seepage, thirty-eight miners were drowned, and it took eight days to rescue the remaining twenty-three men. The sights that Cronin witnessed during his six years in the Welsh valleys were to haunt him for the rest of his life and in time provided the inspiration for his famous novel, *The Stars Look Down*. This story of the unrelentingly grim life of some Northumbrian miners who also suffer a pit disaster was the basis of the second of Cronin's works to be adapted for television, in 1975. Granada made a thirteen-part series of hour long episodes, scripted by Alan Plater and starring Norman Jones, James Bate, Rod Cuthbertson and Avril Elgar.

In 1926, Cronin and his family enjoyed their first experience of real comfort when he moved to London and began practising in Bayswater. Here his patients ranged from some of the poorest members of society to the richest, but in those days before the advent of the National Health Service he developed a real antipathy towards those spoilt patients

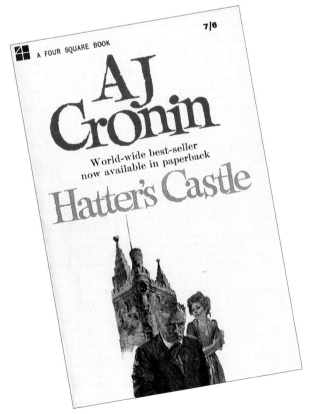

The original NEL paperback editions of Hatter's Castle...

with imaginary illnesses who used their money to waste his time. Indeed, he confessed later to having administered many a harmless solution to satisfy some of these clients and then charged them a large fee!

Eventually, a mixture of dissatisfaction with his work and a diagnosis that the stomach pains he was suffering were being caused by a duodenal ulcer brought about by his long hours of work, made him decide to move with his family back to his native Scotland. And it was in the peace and quiet of the Western Highlands that Cronin, to use his own words, 'followed my natural bent and devoted myself to writing'.

Despite the well-known story that he came close to abandoning his first novel, *Hatter's Castle*, out of exasperation, he actually began by writing serial fiction for a number of popular magazines. Indeed, a number of these stories were later reissued – somewhat to his annoyance – after he had achieved fame and prosperity. He became, in fact, a prodigiously fast and methodical writer who once said he liked to average 5,000 words a day and worked out the plot of every story in advance, down to the last detail.

What is undisputed is that Cronin knew nothing about book publishers, and it was by the merest chance that his wife Mary decided that her husband's story of the retribution which overtakes a despotic Glasgow industrialist should be sent to the London firm of Victor Gollancz Ltd, as Ruth Dudley Edwards has explained in her biography, *Victor Gollancz* (1987):

'Cronin's wife had stuck a pin in a list of publishers and the typescript had gone to Gollancz. The readers had spotted it as a

godsend and Victor had done the rest, throwing everything he knew into a March launch that made Cronin rich and famous overnight.'

The success of *Hatter's Castle* exceeded Cronin's wildest dreams. What other first book by an unknown author could boast of being chosen by the Book Society as their 'Book of the Month' and in so doing ensure sales of at least 30,000 copies? As Cronin himself was later to comment euphorically, 'I thereafter hung up my stethoscope and put away my little black bag – my medical days were over.'

But AJ was also a canny man, as Ruth Dudley Edwards has observed:

'Cronin, once his fourth book, The Citadel, *had outstripped in popularity even* Hatter's Castle, *ceased to question his own talent*

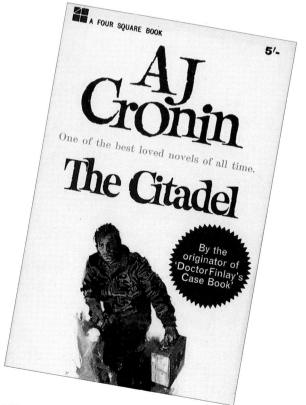

...and The Citadel.

The modern landscape of Callander, setting of the original Dr Finlay's Casebook *as the fictitious 'Tannochbrae'.*

and concentrated more on the small print of Gollancz's contracts. Neither man really liked the other and despite their ostensibly sincere exchanges, they had good reason for mutual distrust. Certainly Victor was privately unenthusiastic about Cronin's books. They stayed together for decades for commercial reasons.'

The Citadel, which appeared in 1937, was undoubtedly the most heartfelt of AJ's novels as well as the most successful. According to another expert on publishing history, Sheila Hodges, the book was the biggest seller in Gollancz's history. In it, Cronin advocated a free public health service in order to defeat the wiles of those Harley Street doctors who 'raised guinea-snatching and the bamboozling of patients to an art form'. Because he knew precisely what he was talking about from his

days in Bayswater, Cronin quickly made a number of powerful enemies in the medical profession and there was a concerted effort by one group of specialists to get *The Citadel* banned. This controversy, of course, only made it more appealing to the general public, and it is claimed that for several months in 1937 the book was being reprinted at the rate of 10,000 copies per week.

Like *The Stars Look Down*, *The Citadel* has also been adapted for television by the BBC, in 1983, as a six-part series. Scripted by Don Shaw and starring Ben Cross and Clare Higgins, the version was well received by both viewers and critics, and according to TV historian Philip Purser, 'launched a minor vogue for serials, preferably about idealistic young doctors from popular novels of the chain library era such as *Sorrell and Son* (1984) and *My Brother Jonathan* (1985)'.

The wide appeal of each of Cronin's nineteen novels made him undeniably one of the most popular novelists of the Forties, Fifties and Sixties, and firmly established him with that other élite band of medical men who had abandoned their profession for the world of literature and there enjoyed great success: writers such as Anton Chekhov, Sir Arthur Conan Doyle and Somerset Maugham. Although his stories were sometimes accused of being unduly melodramatic and old-fashioned, few could match his skill as a storyteller and it is a sign of the enduring appeal of his work that virtually all of his titles are still in print today.

Cronin's books have also been translated into almost two dozen languages, and readers were still anxious for more titles when what proved to be his last novel, *The Minstrel Boy*, about the return of a young priest to his native Eire after many years in Spain, was issued in 1975. When he died on 6 January 1981, at a Swiss clinic in Montreux, AJ had reached the age of eighty-four and left behind an enviable body of popular novels.

Although *Hatter's Castle* may have been the most remarkable of literary débuts;

AJ Cronin, aged seventy-five, at home in Switzerland where he built up an impressive art collection.

The Stars Look Down the most moving and poignant novel of a mining community; and *The Citadel* one of the biggest selling novels of its time, it is Dr Finlay, the TV character based on himself from the pages of *Adventures in Two Worlds*, who has undoubtedly ensured AJ Cronin his most lasting fame. Yet, truth to tell, the omens for the BBC TV series which was only intended as a stopgap in the programme schedules of 1962, were very far from promising.

Chapter Three

THE SECRETS OF THE
ORIGINAL CASEBOOK

HE VAGARIES OF MEMORY and the selective interpretations of the national press have combined to create a number of misconceptions about the original *Dr Finlay's Casebook* which are now firmly entrenched in legend although they are, in fact, quite untrue.

The first of these is that the *Casebook*

was always a Sunday evening series. In fact, for its first two years it went out on Thursday nights. The second is that it was made in Scotland, while for the most of its nine years it was actually transmitted live from the BBC's London studios with filmed location inserts from Callander, the setting for the mythical village of Tannochbrae. Thirdly, it is widely believed that the series was only ever seen in black and white when in truth the final season was made in colour.

Perhaps the most remarkable fact of all is that the programme, launched in 1962 and remembered as one of the most successful and long-running series on television as well as being a landmark in drama serials, was originally planned as a six-parter for early winter evening viewing and had to be hastily brought forward into the summer schedules to fill an embarrassing gap suddenly discovered by the BBC's programme planning department. The records in the BBC archives also indicate that the series was very nearly not produced at all and until the last minute it remained touch-and-go whether the actual episodes would be made, let alone transmitted.

On the face of it, the decision to make *Dr Finlay's Casebook* in the early years of an era that would become known as the 'Swinging Sixties', was a curious one. Here was an unashamedly nostalgic story set in the Twenties about two doctors in a small rural Scottish community, which its proposers were planning to screen at a time when the nation was consumed by interest in the clash of the two Superpowers, the dawning of a new era in fashion, art and music, and rapid developments in space exploration.

Stars of the original Casebook: *Bill Simpson as Dr Finlay, Andrew Cruickshank as Dr Cameron and Barbara Mullen as Janet.*

In the previous year, 1961, for instance, John F Kennedy had become the youngest President of the United States; the Soviet Union had put the first man in space; and the infamous Berlin Wall had been erected between East and West Germany. Early 1962 saw the emergence of a group from Liverpool known as The Beatles, and the first public exhibitions of two new American 'pop artists', Andy Warhol and Roy Lichtenstein. On 11 July, Telstar was launched, which at a stroke made possible live TV broadcasts across the Atlantic. From America, pictures of the chairman of the company which had built the communications satellite were beamed to Europe, while France responded with scenes of actor-singer Yves Montand. Britain's contribution – somewhat delayed because the tracking station at Goonhilly in Cornwall had trouble locking on to Telstar – was a test card and an official greeting.

On Britain's TV screens that year, however, the BBC had already begun to break new ground with a controversial weekly satirical show, *That Was The Week That Was*, and a gritty police drama, *Z-Cars*. Alongside these innovative programmes, technological developments in broadcasting as a whole were also offering a new vision of the future and the race was soon on between the BBC and ITV – which had come into existence in 1955 – to bring this new space age into every living room. It was against this background that *Dr Finlay's Casebook* began its uncertain gestation and unlikely success.

According to documents on file in the BBC's archives in Caversham, the first suggestion for a dramatic serial derived from AJ Cronin's autobiography, *Adventures in Two Worlds*, was floated in 1960 in a letter to the Corporation from two independent programme makers, Henry Cass and Graham Stewart. The idea was considered by Donald Wilson, the head of script development, who had immediate reservations about its 'sloppy romantic approach', but felt it might work *if* the right actors could be found.

The records also show that Cronin was approached about the idea and gave it his cautious blessing. In a subsequent letter he also suggested the name for the central character: Finlay Hyslop. However, negotiations between the various parties appear to have broken down shortly afterwards and the whole project could so easily have joined the many other aborted programme ideas which can still be found cluttering the Caversham files.

But somehow the idea refused to die, and before long another proposal from a different source, titled 'Alec Finlay MD', found its way on to the desk of the BBC script editor, Donald Bull. He was quite unimpressed, as an internal memo clearly indicates: 'Cronin's writings seem to me pulp of a fairly low order, sentimental and insipid and containing every cliché known to medical science, and written in a style reminiscent of Hollywood background music. The characterization is black and white, the plot turns everlastingly foreseeable. A direct translation of such material is out of key with the alertness of present-day audiences.'

Such a damning indictment might well have condemned Finlay to oblivion once and for all. But Donald Bull did add a rider that the stories might possibly work as 'period dramas'. He said that the period detail of Cronin's story was 'three quarters of its charm' because of 'the sense it gives of looking back to a less complex world'.

Further BBC documentation suggests that after some further script conferences, in which all Cronin's novels were considered, an outline emerged for a three-part drama series which mirrored the doctor's own experiences. Finlay's adventures would begin in Wales, to

Dr. FINLAY'S CASEBOOK - TANNOCHBRAE

be followed by him travelling the world as a ship's doctor. In the third, he would be established in a rural Scottish practice.

During the winter of 1961, one of the BBC's most experienced scriptwriters, John Keir Cross, laboured with the concept, but came to the conclusion that it would not work. In a letter to Donald Bull he explained: 'Whichever way I turn I come back to old Cronin. Read anything he writes and the instantaneous impact is effective. His cunning as a writer lies in a kind of alchemy of sheer immediacy. It doesn't bear analysis – but it isn't meant to. For all the rubbish that we, in our bones, know the stuff ought to be, it still commands a worldwide sale.'

Cross had reached the inescapable conclusion that if Finlay, Dr Cameron and Janet were going to be adapted for the screen, they

Dr Finlay's Casebook put the small Perthshire town of Callander firmly on the tourist map.

had to be faithful to the originals. 'I think the Cronin project, in a translation for the screen that observes his own terms, would find its own kind of simple popularity,' he wrote, and added: 'I think, *en passant*, of my typist – a simple person in many ways, but in others, a curiously perceptive and certainly ardent viewer – who dissolved in happy tears when working on the script. She also rejoices in the very conventionalized 'pawkiness' of old Cameron (which may worry us, but that is Cameron's secret) the recurring characteristics of a character rather than any kind of exploration of the character. It was even the way

Dickens works, and is the tried and true formula of the Perry Mason series.'

Although nagging doubts still persisted at the BBC, the project was allowed to continue with the focus remaining on the three central characters as they had been drawn in Cronin's autobiography. The magazine short stories he had written under the collective title, *The Adventures of a Black Bag*, were also utilized. From these sources the characters finally seen on television gradually emerged: Finlay, 'a raw young man, the son of poor farming parents, who grimly and penuriously worked his way to final graduation as a doctor', Dr Cameron, 'a crusty, but likeable old GP', and Janet, 'a stock figure of folksy Scottish stories'. The stories were to be set in Tannochbrae, 'a small town not far from Glasgow'.

It seems possible – even probable – that *Dr Finlay's Casebook* still might never have reached the screen had not the schedulers discovered in the spring of 1962 that they had an unexpected 50-minute gap in their early Thursday evening schedule from the middle of August. Hastily, a stopgap was sought and after a number of partly-developed projects had been considered, the choice fell on *Dr Finlay's Casebook*. It was a brave decision, but one that would so unexpectedly turn an unpretentious six-part series into a roaring nine-year success story (clocking up a total of 206 episodes), make its three stars international celebrities, and finally become a television cult that has been fondly remembered in the public imagination for thirty years.

But back in 1962 time was, of course, of the essence, and initially there were only the outlines for six episodes. Nor did the problem end there. A production team had to be set up, a location for the doctors' practice had to be found and, even more importantly, the three central characters had to be cast.

Campbell Logan, a much-admired veteran producer of Scottish origins, was the man confronted with the task of working a television miracle. 'Originally there were going to be six dramatizations screened some time in the winter,' Logan said, after the launching of the series. 'But then the planners told me these had to be brought forward to August. This left the contracted writers only five weeks to prepare their adaptations. Everything else from set building to hiring the directors and actors had to be rushed forward, too.'

Logan, who had already worked for the BBC for almost twenty-five years and had an enviable record as a drama producer, was probably one of the few men in the Corporation who could have made this almost impossible schedule work. A canny Scot in the same mould as AJ Cronin, he also had an uncanny and important knack of picking the right people for his team.

'I had already made up my mind about the couple to play Dr Cameron and Janet,' he explained. 'I was familiar with the work of Andrew Cruikshank and Barbara Mullen and knew they were just right for the parts. The problem was always going to be Dr Finlay himself. But fate has a way of playing a hand in these sorts of situations. I auditioned a number of young Scots actors who were working in London, and among them was Bill Simpson. He had the right look for a GP and so I just decided to take a gamble.'

The gamble to offer the role of arguably the most important character in the series to an unknown bit-part player was not the only one Campbell took that traumatic summer. 'Bill Simpson wasn't the only completely unknown quantity in the series,' he also admitted later. 'Because of the time element, many of our usual drama directors were already booked, so I had to pick three directors who had never worked in TV before. I think what they have

achieved speaks for itself.'

The three men – Cedric Messina, Gerald Blake and Bill Slater – in fact all played important roles in giving the *Casebook* its sense of period and characterization. And, apart from directing later episodes, the trio subsequently enjoyed long and successful careers in television. Cedric Messina, in par-

Bill Simpson and Barbara Mullen during rehearsals for the Casebook.

ticular, was for many years in charge of the BBC's 'Play of the Month' series, and was also the originator of the BBC Television Shakespeare project.

But despite all the potential problems (for example, the set of Dr Cameron's sitting room in the BBC's Riverside Studios in Hammersmith had to be finished so hurriedly there was no time to install a window) the first episode went out at 7.55 pm on Thursday, 16 August 1962. It was an evening when a medical story had already made the headlines: Dr Maurice Lecutier, a pathologist, stated at an inquest in Chesterfield that a drug named Thalidomide taken by housewife Mrs Ivy Shaw (18), had almost certainly caused the disorder which was followed by the death of her five-month-old baby, Wilfred, who had been born without arms or legs. On the sporting front, viewers had earlier been able to watch a live broadcast of the first day of the Fifth Test against Pakistan in which Colin Cowdrey and Ted Dexter had achieved the highest score for a day's test cricket since 1954 (406–2); while immediately preceding the new programme there had been the latest episode of *Compact*, the popular series about life in a magazine office.

As was traditional, the *Radio Times* ran a short feature about *Dr Finlay's Casebook* and its hero, whose name had now been settled as Alan Finlay: 'Of all the doctors who have written about their calling, AJ Cronin has undoubtedly made the greatest impact. And tonight, this world-famous author reaches his largest audience yet as BBC-TV presents the first episode in a new series based on his stories, *The Adventures of a Black Bag*.

Outlining the plot of the first episode, 'It's All In The Mind' by Vincent Tilsley, the *Radio Times* added:

'The year is 1928 and the place Glasgow. Alan Finlay, a hard-up young medical student with a passionate ambition to become a surgeon, is only a few weeks away from his final exams when he becomes involved in the strange disappearance of his landlady's husband. Finlay, with all the confidence of a student, ventures an opinion, and by chance finds himself in conflict with the veteran, Dr Cameron. It is a chance which is to shape his career.'

The BBC files at Caversham reveal that the Corporation carried out a selected poll among viewers the next day to discover their reactions to the new series. Over 59 per cent gave it an A-rating, most found the story 'very human', while everyone agreed the setting was 'pleasantly old-fashioned'. The omens for the second series were summed up by the one word, 'possible'.

Several episodes were to be screened before a newspaper critic joined in the general public's acclaim for the series. He was Dennis Potter, now one of Britain's most versatile and controversial TV playwrights, and then the TV critic of the *Daily Herald*.

'The crackling fire makes the shadows jump around the room and the oil lamps gleam against pictures on the wall,' he wrote in typically colourful fashion. *'Here we have the domestic detail and social trappings of an earlier decade – the ingredients which are cleverly mixed with the tension of a big hospital series in the BBC show,* Dr Finlay's Casebook. *This Scottish series has plenty of melodrama, but is softened by the authenticity of setting and dignified cadences of dialogue. It is worthy, too, for the fine acting by Andrew Cruikshank as Dr Cameron and Bill Simpson as Dr Finlay.'* Potter urged the BBC: *'Let's see more of* Dr Finlay!'

A week later, the *Daily Express* ventured the opinion that 'the stories by AJ Cronin have atmosphere, credibility and humour; while

Stewart Lane of the *Daily Worker* saw a deeper importance: 'These stories go beyond the theme of a young idealistic doctor's struggles against bureaucracy and superstition to reflect much of the low living standards and the vicious exploitation of the past.'

Statistical records indicate that the series was viewed by eight million viewers in the first week and this rapidly rose to twelve million. Overnight, the BBC had a surprise success almost the equal of ITV's *Coronation Street* (which averaged fourteen million viewers), and it is small wonder that the planners immediately ordered Campbell Logan to extend the six episodes to twelve.

When interviewed again in the late Sixties, Campbell Logan said that he had been confident that *Dr Finlay's Casebook* would indeed be a success – although he certainly did not expect it to run for so long. He was also quick to acknowledge the hard work of the three leading stars and the appeal which the little community of Callander gave the series in doubling as Tannochbrae. (Those viewers of a motoring frame of mind probably found the veteran cars belonging to the two doctors almost equally appealing: Dr Cameron's 1928 'Bullnose' Morris and Dr Finlay's sporty 1913 Sunbeam Tourer which he later replaced with a 1925 Wolseley.) 'Its popularity is built on good character drawing,' Logan reflected, 'and on good psychology; also on sentiment which never turns into sentimentality.'

The success of the *Casebook* inevitably led to a second series – which was again shown on Thursday evenings; but it was not until 1964 that it was moved to the night with which it has forever been associated: Sunday. Even then, it was not aired until 9 pm. Nor was this success story just restricted to the United Kingdom, for apart from being transmitted in such obvious places as America (from PBS in Boston), and via the Canadian Broadcasting Corporation and Australian Broadcasting Corporation, it was also seen in Kenya, Nigeria, Uganda, Hong Kong, Ghana, Sierra Leone, Pakistan, Zambia, Poland and several other non-English-speaking countries.

Many elements undoubtedly contributed to the appeal of the series, though few individual episodes are better remembered than 'Spotless Reputation', which was screened on 25 October 1962, as the world teetered on the edge of nuclear war during the Cuban Missile Crisis. In the *Dr Finlay* story, the pair of doctors had become involved in the lives of two quite different men: a Cockney shopkeeper and a rich, titled Scots businessman. Both men seemed worlds apart, but thanks to the intervention of the two GPs they were shown to have a lot in common, both as patients and parents. Parallels with the real-life confrontation between the Soviet leader Khrushchev and US President Kennedy were painfully apparent; however, the depiction of solid human virtues triumphing against the background of a vivid dramatic situation also seemed very apposite.

Apart from good stories, strong characterization, humour and pathos (not overlooking a faithful representation of the period), the series struck other, unexpected chords in the 'Swinging Sixties'. The characters were all seen as being solid and trustworthy with a sense of their responsibility towards the community. Yet the series was never accused of being bland, and confrontations between the two doctors were always a strong element in the sub-plots. As Julian Critchley later wrote in *The Times*, in February 1969:

'*The relationship between Finlay and Cameron is one in which Finlay tilts at windmills only to be rescued by Cameron, whose knowledge of Freud may not be*

THE SECRETS OF THE ORIGINAL CASEBOOK

(Opposite) Andrew Cruickshank joins Bill Simpson and Barbara Mullen for a rehearsal of a kitchen scene, at the London Studios.

great but whose instinct for people Finlay cannot match. It is a victory for age in a medium where youth can appear to be the only qualification.'

The second series of *Dr Finlay's Casebook* was launched on Thursday, 5 September 1963, with rather more fanfare than its predecessor. Michael Gowers of the *Daily Mail* greeted it with fulsome praise: 'The migration has begun – but if one swallow doesn't make a summer, the return of *Dr Finlay's Casebook* hard on the heels of *Z-Cars* is a certain indication that television's march into the high season is under way.'

The series generated a warmth and a charm which were rare commodities, Gowers continued, and he said of the leading actors: 'Here is a trio which would be hard to match and a concentration on character always reflected in the delightful lilt of the dialogue… Set beside the white-coated nonentities in the television of the Welfare State, these people recall the days of paper and string medicine when a doctor was not only a doctor but had time to be a personal friend as well.'

But this was a view not shared by at least one doctor who, the following April, wrote to the journal *GP* complaining that the image of the family doctor as presented in *Dr Finlay's Casebook* lacked the glamour of other medical series. He claimed that all TV medical programmes tended to disparage the role of the general practitioner and glamorize hospital medicine, especially in some of the

newer series like *Emergency Ward 10* and the American import, *Dr Kildare*. 'But does the poor old GP get glamour programmes showing him dashing about, dramatically saving people's lives?' the anonymous practitioner asked. 'Oh dear no! We get Dr Finlay and dear old Dr Cameron, of course. But the subtle inference is that they are a couple of comics representing a bygone age.'

Undoubtedly, most of the programme's other millions of viewers did not share this view, but by this time there were a few signs that the series was not pleasing some people. Among these was AJ Cronin himself. Although AJ could obviously not watch the series in Switzerland, he was sent copies of all scripts to comment upon. He remained happy with these until 1964, when (the BBC archives reveal) he wrote a blunt letter to the series' script editor, Harry Green:

'Incidents have progressively departed from my original conceptions. They are relevant neither to the characterizations nor the background, but are simply unrelated, extraneous events dragged in, often sensationally, and with little or no bearing on the realities of medical practice in a Scottish village. Of course, there is a wide audience of sorts for soap opera, but who wants this?'

Word of Cronin's displeasure leaked to the media and in June 1964, stories appeared in the national press suggesting the author had 'had enough and wanted the series to end'. He would not sanction the BBC to make any more *Dr Finlay's Casebook*, it was stated.

The outcry from the viewing public was immediate. Sackfuls of mail were despatched to Switzerland and one newspaper even accused the author of 'maliciously doing millions out of legitimate enjoyment.' Cronin was, of course, no stranger to controversy, having been attacked by the medical profession and the press in the past over his book, *The Citadel.* He decided, nonetheless, to issue a statement to refute the charges made against him.

> *'I have had hundreds of letters from viewers saying how sorry they were that the series was ending and that they were sorry that I was to blame,'* he said on 7 June. *'I don't like to disappoint anybody, but just lately the series has got out of line. The scripts have been getting ragged and introduced extraneous characters. If you overrun a programme, you end up with a soap opera. What annoys me is that the BBC have placed the whole onus of the row on me. I have written telling them it is a matter of improving scripts. I have no intention of stopping the series. I merely want a longer break than they have suggested before the next series.'*

If anything, this temporary spat only served to increase the popularity of *Dr Finlay's Casebook,* and *The Times* declared with considerable presentiment, as the last episode of the third series was being screened in July 1964: *'Dr Finlay* promises to attain immortality.'

In 1965, the rivalry for audiences between *Dr Finlay's Casebook* and *Dr Kildare,* the fifty-minute American series with Richard Chamberlain as a young intern and Raymond Massey as his gruff old adviser, really began to hot up. Indeed, before the series returned to the screen, the new producer, Gerard Glaister, promised that it would be 'a little less coy' with 'more social awareness'. Once back, however, the general consensus among the British critics was that the home-grown production was far more worthwhile than the American import, as Adrian Mitchell wrote in the *Sun* of 15 February:

> *'If you compare* Dr Finlay *to* Dr Kildare, *its virtues positively shine. The American series tends to come to neat and morally-comfortable conclusions. The Scots series ends, like any sentence spoken by a Fifeshire man, with a question mark. Kildare's humour is heavy and manufactured; Finlay's is pawky and homespun. And the* Casebook *doesn't rely for its glamour upon the picturesque crags of Andrew Cruikshank's face, but on cunningly-inserted views of Scottish landscape.'*

The series also showed that it was quite willing to tackle controversial subjects: an episode in April in which Finlay almost perjured himself for the sake of a beautiful shoplifter, was followed by still stronger medicine with the story of 'Belle', a backstreet abortionist. The plot revolved around two of Belle's operations that went wrong, causing death in one case and serious illness in the other.

John Woodforde of the *Sunday Telegraph* described it as 'by any standards the best play of the week', and said that the fact it had turned out to be such a *tour de force* was remarkable considering its theme.

> *'Can you imagine the single-play merchants tackling that sort of thing?'* he enquired. *'And if they did, what an outcry about bad taste would follow. Just as nearly all* Dr Finlay *episodes are models of the beginning-middle-end genre, so "Belle" was a double object lesson, in that the play brought excitement and interest out of squalid doings without resort to sensationalism.'*

If the BBC had any fears that viewers might find such stories distasteful, despite the comforting presence of the two doctors, they certainly received no complaints. And as if to further underline the show's evident sense of responsibility, in November 1965 it was one of just a handful to be publicly condoned by Mary Whitehouse, the 'Clean Up TV Campaigner', when she announced the formation of the National Viewers and Listeners Association to tackle 'BBC bad taste and irresponsibility'.

There were occasional eccentric voices of complaint, though. In November 1965, for instance, the Reverend John R Gray told the first meeting of the Church of Scotland Total Abstainers Association that any country doctor who drank as much as Dr Finlay did, would have long since lost his practice. Andrew Cruikshank came immediately to the defence of his partner. 'We certainly look forward to a small whisky before the evening meal, or late at night before going to bed, as a sort of sustainer. After all, Finlay does not smoke and Cameron only smokes a pipe. They live terribly ascetic lives.'

Dr Finlay's Casebook was now in every sense a cult – even a national institution. That same year, a Bill Simpson Fan Club was set up. A record about *Dr Finlay* sung by Andy Stewart, was in the Hit Parade for five weeks, while Andrew Cruikshank was a guest of honour at the annual dinner of the British Medical Association, where he was invited to speak on medical matters for all the world as if he was a real GP.

The series also began to enlarge the roles of some of its minor characters when they caught the public fancy: the artful Dr Snoddie, for example, played with insinuating glee by Eric Woodburn, or Effie Morrison as the district nurse, Mistress Niven, with her tongue of brass and heart to match. Even to introduce wholly new characters such as Dr Finlay's father, an irascible old man who was played with great gusto by the veteran radio star, Wilfred Pickles. Among other well-known names who guested on the series

Alfred Marks (as Dr Gilbert, in 'The Quack'); Patrick Troughton as Alex Dean, the gardener at Arden House; and Jane Asher, as Mattie Lennox, one of Dr Finlay's 'young ladies'.

Philip Purser in the *Sunday Telegraph*, however, chose the episode featuring old man Finlay to deliver a stinging attack on his son. Though he conceded that the role of Dr Finlay was still being 'brilliantly played by Bill Simpson', he thought the GP was now 'slackening, thickening, greying, despite efforts to stimulate the youthful impetuosity he first brought to Tannochbrae. He is in fact smug, self-satisfied, self-righteous. He is also a bully. He is now one of the few utterly detestable characters in television.'

Even such an uncompromising attack – which brought Purser a shoal of protests – could not dampen the enthusiasm which surrounded the screening of the 100th episode on 16 April 1966. Nancy Banks-Smith in the *Sun* marked the centenary with a congratulatory telegram, as well as a salutary warning:

> '*Dr Finlay's Casebook is still gentle, unpretentious and faithful,*' she wrote. '*It's also eternally restricted to being gentle, unpretentious and faithful. Last night's episode about Dr Finlay dipping yet another tentative toe into the inconceivable sea of matrimony was a case in point. He can never marry. Or Cameron die. Or Janet leave. Though they all threaten to time and again. Arden House is a daguerreotype which cannot change or progress, but only, in the natural course of things, fade.*'

Despite such comments, however, the series returned once more in October 1967. Peter Knight, of the *Daily Telegraph*, who shared none of the opinion of his colleague, took the opportunity to record another small triumph for the series:

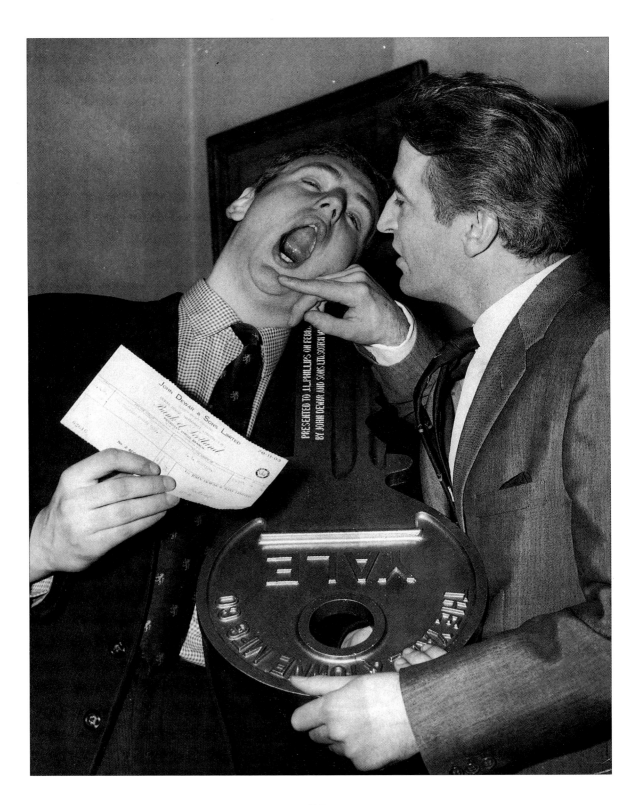

(Opposite) *Bill Simpson jokingly examines a medical student's throat when handing him first prize in a whisky drinkers competition, in 1966.*

'With the passing from the small screen of all the other high-powered modern medicos, Dr Finlay's Casebook *is now the sole survivor in this once fertile field of TV drama. It has outstripped all its rivals without ever having changed its style. Unlike its competitors, the medical content here merely provides a background against which the human dramas are worked out.'*

Nothing, it seemed, could deflect the affection in which the series was held by its faithful fans, whose numbers still exceeded eleven million. Nor did the advent of colour television, introduced by the BBC in the autumn of 1967 (ITV followed two years later), threaten this popularity.

Indeed, the true stature of *Dr Finlay's Casebook* was finally acknowledged in March 1969: those same planners who pulled the embryo series forward to fill a weekday gap decided it was the only show to fill the 7.25 pm slot left by *The Forsyte Saga* when that legendary twenty-six-part drama involving a family of London merchants which had gripped the nation came to its end. With the demise of the despotic Soames (Eric Porter) and his hapless wife Irene (Nyree Dawn Porter) as essential Sunday evening viewing, Finlay, Cameron, Janet and the folk of Tannochbrae were chosen to maintain the advantage the BBC had gained over ITV through another twenty-six-part season. Once again, the series did not fail its makers. Maurice Wiggin writing in *The Sunday Times* after the changeover had occurred, enthused: 'The staying power of *Dr Finlay* is one of the

seven wonders of television.'

This series, however, introduced a dramatic change from its predecessors in allowing Dr Finlay – rather like his creator, AJ Cronin – to take himself off to London and there set himself up in a Mayfair clinic. And if this in itself was not enough, he was also hopelessly beguiled by Barbara, 'a cool temptress', played by Tracy Reed. The attraction between Bill Simpson and his co-star was, in fact, soon being repeated off the set, as certain London newspaper gossip columnists were happy to point out. Indeed, the *Casebook* found itself one of the earliest targets of the kind of tabloid speculation that now regularly fills the front pages of such papers, namely romantic involvements between TV personalities. But Finlay was soon safely back on his way to Tannochbrae, and not just as a result of a campaign run by the *Daily Mirror* to sound out the views of its readers. Perhaps more so because in the opinion of most people, he seemed like a fish out of water in both London and in love.

The twelfth series, which began on 13 September 1970, finally made the transition to colour, giving viewers a chance to see, in full glory, the picturesque scenery around Arden House, and the floral wallpaper, ruby red curtains and dark oak furniture within. The *Daily Express* also recorded that the series 'now threatens to be the longest-running medical operation since Dr Dale.' (This referred to a 1960s long-running radio serial, *Mrs Dale's Diary*, as popular in its day as *The Archers* has now become.)

Although this was, in fact, to prove the last series, it did contain several memorable episodes, especially Clifford Hanley's tense drama about a rapist on the loose in Tannochbrae, and Elaine Morgan's 'Dust', screened just before Christmas when viewers were huddled round their sets as Arctic conditions raged outside.

'Dust' was a story extracted very much from AJ Cronin's experiences with mining. It concerned a local miner, Willie Gallagher (played with enormous conviction by Callum Mill), who returns to Tannochbrae after a meeting with Lenin, determined to campaign for better wages and pensions for his fellow miners, as well as attempting to try and alleviate the menace of silicosis. It was an intensely dramatic episode which did not make easy viewing, but instead vividly depicted the suffering caused to miners by the disease, thus highlighting the meanness of the authorities who were trying to cut down to a minimum the amount spent on compensating silicosis victims.

Jack Sutherland of the *Morning Star* described the episode as 'riveting to watch', and added: 'The deeply moving ending brought together miners, Gallagher and Finlay, and was expressive of the socialist and humanist sympathies of AJ Cronin on whose characters this series is based.'

If Cronin could have asked for Finlay to have made one of his last appearances in any story 'Dust' was surely a good choice, drawing on a subject dear to his heart and for which he, too, had campaigned. It brought tears to many eyes, as did the news that a piece of television history was about to end.

Despite more sacks of letters from viewers, both the BBC and Cronin were now in agreement that the series had run its course. The viewing figures were inevitably starting to fall, and the author reiterated his concern that the programme should not be allowed to degenerate into a soap opera. The very last episode, 'The Burgess Ticket', was screened on Sunday, 3 January 1971. The following week it was replaced by very different fare: the cases of Paul Temple, the detective created by Francis Durbridge, who had been on the radio for almost thirty years and who now made his debut on TV in 'House of Dread', starring John Bentley.

Since its finale, *Dr Finlay's Casebook,* with its unique combination of characterization and setting has nevertheless continued to influence many other period series. Indeed, only two years later, in January 1972, Granada TV launched *Adam Smith*, an unashamed though ultimately unsuccessful attempt to revive its spirit and traditions in the story of daily life in a small, isolated Scottish community. Written by Trevor Griffiths, it was even transmitted in the same early Sunday evening slot.

The series starred Andrew Keir as a minister in the village of Lammerton caring for the various needs of his parishioners. The location chosen for the filming was Gifford, a picturesque village in East Lothian, because, producer June Howson admitted at the time, 'We hope it will become as famous as Tannochbrae in *Dr Finlay's Casebook.*'

Although the stories in *Adam Smith* differed in that the kirk replaced the surgery as the focal point, the series did have its own GP, Dr Calvi, who was frequently brought into conflict with the minister when the demands of religion and medicine clashed. The doctor was played by a young actor making his television debut, called Tom Conti. Curiously, twenty years later, when the new *Doctor Finlay* was announced by Scottish Television, Conti would be the first person tipped to play the title role.

(Opposite) *Barbara Mullen and Bill Simpson run through a script together.*

Chapter Four

THE FILE ON DOCTOR FINLAY

T HE DISTANCE BETWEEN GLASGOW and the small Fifeshire town, with the unlikely-sounding name of Auchtermuchty, is about sixty miles by road. The journey from the modernized sprawl of Glasgow via Kincardine, the higher reaches of the Firth of Forth, and along the lower slopes of the Ochil Hills to 'Muchty (as the locals refer to their community), takes about ninety minutes by car, but enables the traveller to pass from the heart of industrial Scotland to a stretch of countryside still locked in the time warp of an earlier age.

Although there are several stretches of motorway which now make driving much easier through Stirling, Kinross and Fife towards the east coast, the traveller becomes increasingly aware of the traditional, rolling country farmland and clutches of grey, stone-walled houses which represent an earlier time when life was harder, but arguably more satisfying, and certainly less hectic than today. It is a journey that I made in the summer of 1993 to discover the story behind the making of Scottish Television Enterprises' *Doctor Finlay*.

My trip began in the independent TV company's stylish modern headquarters in Cowcaddens (where the idea for the series was conceived) and then took me to little Auchtermuchty which has been transformed, by skill and subterfuge, into the centre of Finlay's rural practice: the fictional town of Tannochbrae. As my host and guide, I had the man closest to the making of this latest television success story, the producer, Peter Wolfes.

Peter, a tall, soft-spoken freelance TV producer with a wry sense of humour and a very clear vision of his job, was hired to mastermind *Doctor Finlay* as a result of his work on a succession of very popular series including *Colditz*, *The Onedin Line* and most recently, *The Bill*.

The original decision to do a new version of *Doctor Finlay* had been made by STE's triumvirate of Alistair Moffat, at the time Director of Programmes and now Chief Executive of the Company, Gus MacDonald, Scottish Television's Managing Director, and Robert Love, Controller of Drama. Once they had acquired the television rights to *Finlay* from the BBC (who had, to their surprise, allowed them to lapse), STE found it was no problem selling the programme to the ITV network. Robert Love, at this stage, discussed with Bill Craig (who was working on the scripts) the idea of setting the new *Doctor Finlay* in a post-war Scottish town and introducing a new character, the headstrong young Dr Neil. Once the concept had been agreed and scripts commissioned, Robert Love invited Peter Wolfes to join the team as producer, working closely on the scripts with Patrick Lau, the director, Pamela Wilson, the Script Executive, and the writers themselves.

Given a budget of £3.5 million by STE

Is Dr Finlay bound for Callander?

THE PEOPLE of Callander have expressed their delight over the possibility that Dr Finlay is about to reopen his television casebook.

The Trossachs tourist town was the setting for the popular Dr Finlay's Casebook, filmed for seven years during the 60s.

Now, with original makers BBC selling off the rights to the programme, Scottish Television are planning a new production of the series with Callander a strong candidate for location work.

"It will be a tremendous boost for the town if they do bring Dr Finlay's casebook back to Callander," said Mr Callum Gray, whose baker's shop was used in an episode of the original series.

"Callander is very much a tourist town and for years after the programme finished people from all over would come and ask to see where everything took place," Mr Gray went on.

"In fact they still do, so it can mean nothing but good for the whole place."

At present the new programme is still in the very early planning stages but already the names of actors have been put forward as suitable replacements for the 60s cast.

Television insiders believe Crieff-born Tom Conti is ready to take on Bill Simpson's lead role of Dr Finlay while Maggie Smith, star of The Prime of Miss Jean Brodie, is rated as perfect for the part of housekeeper Janet.

One very hopeful suggestion reckoned superstar Sean Connery would have ideal qualities for the character of pipe-smoking Dr Cameron, originally played by Andrew Cruikshank.

"If he does take the part the people of Callander will be voting for home rule within days," joked resident Jim Maguire in reference to Mr Connery's highly publicised political views.

Although STV producers would have little difficulty in winning the favour of locals when filming a problem they could face is the much-changed nature of Callander itself.

Many of the buildings used over 25 years ago could not fit into Dr Finlay's 1920s setting because they have been modernised. Others have simply been demolished.

A row of small cottages in Pearl Street, prominent in the series, were knocked down long ago, along with the railway station.

One particular sticking point for STV could be the siting of Dr Finlay's home, Arden House, originally picked by the production crew after a suggestion from their chauffeur, local man Alastair Cameron.

It is now run as a guest house under the name Arden House and owners Jim and Dorothy McGregor are uncertain whether they will allow a film crew into their p̶ ̶ ̶ ̶ ̶ advertisi̶ ̶ ̶ ̶ the hom̶ ̶ ̶ ̶ ̶ ̶ ̶

Casebook.

"As yet there has been no official approach from STV and, until there is, we have no idea what any filming would involve," said Dorothy McGregor.

"We would have absolutely no objection to any filming from outside," she ̶ ̶ ̶ ̶ ̶ on.

ourselves as a quiet place to stay and I would hate to think our guests would be disrupted by a camera crew sprawled all over the place," she added.

A spokesman for STV said Dr Finlay's Casebook was one of a number of programme options currently under review and planning was still at an early stage.

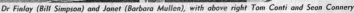

Dr Finlay (Bill Simpson) and Janet (Barbara Mullen), with above right Tom Conti and Sean Connery.

Tannochbrae revisited: press speculation on the new Dr Finlay in early 1992.

and asked to make a new series as popular as Scottish Television's ratings-winner, *Taggart*, he has reinvented a legend and built a team of actors and technicians whose compatibility and skill is there for all to see at work and, more particularly, to view on the small screen.

Yet despite all Peter's earlier achievements, working on *Doctor Finlay* has had a special poignancy for him, as the original *Casebook* provided him with his first taste of the television drama which has subsequently become the focus of his working life. As we drove from Glasgow to Auchtermuchty on a bright

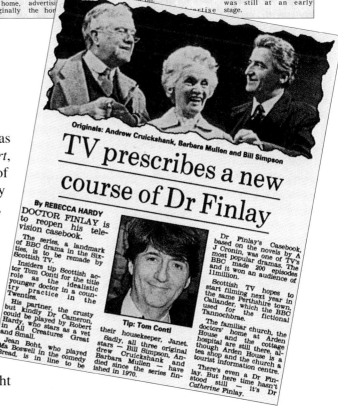

Originals: Andrew Cruickshank, Barbara Mullen and Bill Simpson

TV prescribes a new course of Dr Finlay

By REBECCA HARDY

DOCTOR FINLAY is to reopen his television casebook.

The series, a landmark of BBC drama in the Sixties, is to be remade by Scottish TV.

Insiders tip Scottish actor Tom Conti for the title role as the idealistic younger doctor in a country practice in the Twenties.

His partner, the crusty but kindly Dr Cameron, could be played by Robert Hardy, who stars as a vet in All Creatures Great and Small.

Jean Boht, who played Ma Boswell in the comedy Bread, is in line to be

Tip: Tom Conti

their housekeeper, Janet.

Sadly, all three original stars — Bill Simpson, Andrew Cruickshank and Barbara Mullen — have died since the series finished in 1970.

Dr Finlay's Casebook, based on the novels by A J Cronin, was one of TV's most popular dramas. The BBC made 200 episodes and it won an audience of 11 million.

Scottish TV hopes to start filming next year in the same Perthshire town, Callander, which the BBC used for the fictional Tannochbrae.

The familiar church, the doctors' home at Arden House and the cottage hospital are still there, although Arden House is a tea shop and the church a tourist information centre.

There's even a Dr Finlay. But here time hasn't stood still — it's Dr Catherine Finlay.

Peter Wolfes, producer of Doctor Finlay.

Questors, a thriving amateur group in Ealing.

'I was very unsure about what I wanted to do,' he said, as we threaded our way out of Glasgow through the traffic of Bishopbriggs. 'But I knew I didn't want to be an actor. The result was I spent two years at RADA learning stage-management. That led to a couple of years working as a stage-manager in the professional theatre. But there was no money in the theatre in those days (I was earning about £12 per week) and as there was a continual exodus to the new ITV companies which were opening in the late Sixties, I decided to join them. I had a pretty steady job in the Sheffield Playhouse, but you have to remember that there was full employment in those days, so it wasn't quite the gamble it might seem today.

'So, I wrote off to all the names and addresses I could find and, amazingly, the first to reply were the BBC in Glasgow,' Peter recalls, with a smile. 'I thought, "Oh, God, what shall I do?" But then I decided, I've got this far north, it's all an adventure. So I packed all my worldly belongings into my Mini and set off for Glasgow, wondering what on earth I had let myself into.'

Peter soon found himself working as a general trainee (there was, he says, no formal training as such in the BBC at that time) and within days he was being sent off to do things he had no idea about. 'One of my assignments

and (for once) dry August afternoon, he talked to me about his experiences in television, and also the twist of fate that reunited him two decades later with the characters created by AJ Cronin.

The world of television was not something that seemed a likely career for London-born Peter, for his father was a solicitor and wanted him to study the law. However, his mother's side of the family were a little more artistically inclined, Peter remembers, and it was she who was rather more supportive of his interest in the theatre, which had begun during his childhood when he appeared in school plays. It continued when he joined The was with *Grandstand*,' he said. 'I was told that all I had to do was cue Harry Carpenter at the right moment. But *when* was the right moment? Anyhow, Harry Carpenter took not the slightest notice of me standing beside the camera, waving my arms. He was already talking, anyway, and obviously thought, "What is that twit doing?" '

Peter's most amusing mission was to Aberdeen to be floor-manager on a

Peter Wolfes with one of the directors, Patrick Lau, on location.

current affairs programme. What they had omitted to tell him, however, was that the programme was all in Gaelic – naturally, he couldn't understand a word. 'They knew I was green and really just threw me in the deep end, so I had to learn the hard way,' he went on, as on our journey, the built-up areas of Glasgow began to give way to the open countryside. 'After about six months doing all kinds of general television, I plucked up courage and said that what I really wanted to do was work on drama. To my surprise, the BBC agreed and put me on *Dr Finlay's Casebook*, as an assistant floor-manager. The series was then being made in the BBC's Glasgow studios, with the rare outing for location shooting in Callander. That was in 1970.

'Of course, I didn't know at the time that the episodes I worked on were going to be the last. I just remember thinking, "Wow!", and recalling what an event it had been when I had watched the series as a youngster each week. It seemed to me that the whole

population was captivated by the series and the streets were deserted.

'Working on the *Casebook* was quite a change for me, after having been in the theatre and sport, and then in current affairs. I had to learn a whole new set of techniques; the whole process of making programmes was so different.'

The last series of *Dr Finlay's Casebook* was not altogether a happy one, Peter remembers. 'It had been going for seven years and the BBC and everyone connected with it were beginning to get, understandably, a bit weary.

'The really extraordinary thing was that even though we were making the programme at the end of the Sixties, they were still recording each episode in one go: a kind of throwback to the fact that it had used to be live television. They just hadn't been able to kick the habit of doing it all in one day.

'As I recall, we had a week to rehearse and then two days in the studio. We would spend a day and a half on the set rehearsing the whole thing, and then at 7.30 pm on the second night we'd go through it all in an hour. It was like a live play, which was great for everyone in terms of adrenalin, but it meant you only had one chance to get it right. For its time, the *Casebook* was technically very old-fashioned.' Peter paused to indicate out the window our first sight of the Firth of Forth, and then went on: 'Of course, some of the directors on those last episodes complained that it was a ridiculous way to make such a popular drama series. Why couldn't they shoot it one scene at a time, they asked? just as we do now. So it was really not a very sophisticated programme, however fondly people may remember it. To be absolutely fair, though, no television studio drama at that time was very sophisticated, in the way we know TV today. The editing was terribly slow, the cutting was terribly slow, and the performances were very over the top, larger than life and not very real. Despite this, some of the issues which they dealt with were, for the time, quite frank.

'Ironically, the last episode on which I worked – which was the final one of the series – was all made on film. It seemed to breathe new life into everyone, both the actors and the production team. I have sometimes thought since that if only they had decided to carry on using film, they might have been able to keep the series going even longer. The audiences were still there. I assume that everyone had just had enough.'

Peter remains grateful for the experience he gained of drama productions while working on *Dr Finlay's Casebook*; and it certainly stood him in good stead when he moved on to work for two years on another popular BBC Scottish series, *The Borderers* (1969–70), about cattle and sheep rustling in the seventeenth century. This 'northern western', which was produced by Peter Graham Scott, starred Iain Cuthbertson as a cunning warden. The format had been devised by Bill Craig, who was later involved as scriptwriter on *Sunset Song* (1971), a serialization of Lewis Grassic Gibbon's novel about the raw life of north-east Scotland in the nineteenth century, and which also provided Peter Wolfes with his third experience of period drama. The two men were destined to collaborate twenty years later when Bill Craig started to write for *Doctor Finlay*.

Feeling by then that he had 'done his bit for Scotland', Peter returned to London where he worked in the drama series and drama plays departments of the BBC for several years. He was first assistant on a number of series and also on the highly acclaimed 'Play of the Month' production of *A Midsummer Night's Dream* masterminded by Cedric Messina, who had, of course, cut his teeth in TV drama as a director on *Dr Finlay's Casebook*.

Peter's star continued to rise and he was soon facing the even more demanding tasks which confront an assistant director and production manager. A particularly rewarding stint followed as associate producer with Peter Goodchild on a number of controversial productions such as *Oppenheimer* (1981), the story of the American professor who became 'the father of the atomic bomb', and *The Monocled Mutineer* (1985), about a working-class rebel British soldier in the First World War.

Finally, Peter decided to become an independent producer and with his reputation having gone before him, was hired by Thames to make the highly popular police series, *The Bill*. When he again decided to move on, a meeting with Robert Love, the Controller of

BOB MCINTOSH, PRODUCER: A LINK WITH THE PAST...

*B*OB MCINTOSH is one of the few remaining links with the original *Dr Finlay's Casebook* who has lived to see the new series. Now retired and in his seventies, he lives by coincidence at Cupar, a short drive away from Auchtermuchty, on the A9 road to St Andrews. As a former director, and senior drama producer with the BBC in Glasgow until his retirement several years ago, it is hardly surprising that he has shown a keen interest in the making of STE's *Doctor Finlay* and used the opportunity to reminisce about its predecessor.

During his years at the BBC, Bob worked on some of the Corporation's most prestigious drama series including *The Expert* (1970–5) with Marius Goring, about the life of a police patholo-gist, *Sutherland's Law* (1976) the stories of a Scottish procurator fiscal starring Iain Cuthbertson and Desmond Bagley's thriller, *Running Blind*, much of which was filmed in Ireland. Nevertheless, he has a special fondness for *Dr Finlay's Casebook*, which he joined as floor-man-ager in London when it was already a success.

'It was the only series the BBC could use to break the Church deadlock on Sunday showing,' he recalled, in an interview in July 1992. 'It went out after the evening service, but for years the BBC had wanted to get away from that with an earlier show-ing, and the only programme they could get through without affecting the church too much was *Dr Finlay's Casebook*, although it did have a very adverse effect on evening attendances.'

Bob said that the series was 'a lovely one to work on', and the three leading actors became very close to it, as well as to each other. 'Andrew Cruikshank was very much the guiding light,' Bob recalled. 'He was a first class Shakespearean actor, a highly intelligent and likeable man, and a total professional who was respected by all. Barbara was also a great professional who made the role of Janet her own. Bill, a gentle and self-effacing man, quickly became identified as Dr Finlay. They became three of the highest-paid actors in Britain

because the show was so popular, and they certainly earned their money.'

Bob also recalled the relocation of the series from London to Glasgow, which enabled it to take advantage of the new colour facilities at the stu-dios, which were then the first to be available out-side the BBC's headquarters. He, too, moved up the ladder to become a producer's assistant and later the associate producer.

Part of his job was to scout locations in and around Callander, and he has never forgotten the generosity and hospitality of the local people. 'It was very difficult to pay them for the use of their properties,' he says. 'Most people refused, and I often ended up taking along a bunch of flowers and chocolates. Others would ask us to make a contribution to the church funds, instead. They all took the series very much to their hearts, and as far as they were concerned, they *were* Tannochbrae.'

Bob believes part of the reason for the series' success was because it was 'a decent programme, featuring decent people, playing decent characters, which made you feel as if some good was being done'. He thinks that viewers enjoyed both the nos-talgia and the fact that the stories contained themes that were relevant to contemporary issues, such as parental problems, illness and political unrest.

Although he was sad when the series ended in 1971, he believes it finished at the right time, and on a high. His memories of the very last episode, 'The Burgess Ticket', are especially nos-talgic, as he was the director. 'I'd already had some experience directing on *The Troubleshooters* and *Softly, Softly*, so when the producer asked if I would like to direct the final episode of the *Casebook*, I jumped at it,' he said. Once again, we dealt with a contemporary issue – this time alco-holism – but the episode, which was set in 1931, also marked the retirement of Dr Cameron and his being granted the freedom of Tannochbrae. He was presented with a specially-inscribed bound volume and I still have that book as a reminder to this day.'

Drama at STE, once more dramatically changed the course of his career.

The gently undulating peaks of the Ochil Hills were now coming into view through the left-hand windows of the car as Peter described how the GP from Tannochbrae had been brought back into his life again. 'Robert Love invited me to his office and told me that STE were planning to do *Doctor Finlay,* and would I be interested? I said at once, "Oh, yes".' The question I then put to Peter was the same one he had asked himself and has also been asked dozens of times by journalists. *Why* make another series about Dr Finlay?

'I think STE were basically looking for another banker like *Taggart,*' he says frankly. 'My first concern was the "remake syndrome". It is not necessarily the case that you can just pick up where someone left off and continue the success. Having said that, a lot of things do get remade and there is always a way of putting a new interpretation on any story. For example, look at how often *Dracula* has been remade.

'Of course, we have since caught some flack from the press directed at ITV for being a bit lazy. "Why can't you come up with new ideas instead of remaking *Dr Finlay* or *Maigret*?" we were asked. "Why did you have to go back to the past?" It is a difficult argument to counter and I have to admit that, in that kind of climate, I was a bit nervous about doing the series.

'It was then I realized that Finlay has got more going for him than was being discussed,' he continued. 'If you dig a bit deeper you find that AJ Cronin created some very good characters. They are not ready made, but with the right scripts and the right casting they can work.'

Peter digressed for a moment into his own role. 'In fact, these elements in a series such as *Doctor Finlay* are absolutely crucial. You can only have one go at it. You must get the writers and the cast and the directors right. If you don't, you only have yourself to blame.' We passed a sign to the curiously-named Rumbling Bridge and Yetts o' Muckhart. 'So being brought up in the quite tough environment of drama documentaries has given me a kind of fighting edge, I suppose, for the sort of television I like making.' (As I was to discover during the subsequent days I spent with Peter, 'edge' is a word he likes to use when referring to television that attempts to do more than entertain, and encourages audiences to think, too.) 'I thought to myself, "Why not combine the two? You can be entertaining, which is obviously a prime requirement, but also try to sharpen up the characters and give them a reality which wasn't in the earlier series.'

'Even with the benefit of hindsight, the original characters were quite flowery. You never delved into their private lives. You never saw them tussle with emotional difficulties or problems. Subsequently, you never really knew very much about them. They were not superficial, but just very much on the surface. It was the kind of predicaments in which they found themselves, or the events of the day, that would lead you through the story-telling. That was what you would watch, not necessarily, funnily enough, the characters themselves.'

Sensing this problem could arise again, both he and Robert Love knew how tricky it was going to be to get the right cast, and Peter now says he 'dreads to think' what might have been the outcome if any of their quartet of choices for the leading characters had declined to appear. 'There were just no other ideas we were happy with,' he claims.

But what of all the speculation about names which had greeted the announcement that STE were to make *Doctor Finlay*?

Filming of Berlin scenes from the first episode of Doctor Finlay.

'There certainly had been a number of stories before I was appointed as producer,' Peter admits. 'Whether they were leaks or not, I don't know. Robert Love told me that there had been some earlier conversations with Brian Cox, but I didn't think he was right for the part.' (Brian Cox is the Scottish character actor best known on television for his role as Henry II in the updated serial about the Plantagenets, *The Devil's Crown* (1978), and on film as the original Hannibal Lecter in *Manhunter*.) Neither did Peter think that Tom Conti, whose name had also been mentioned by the press, would be right.

'Nevertheless,' he continued, 'one thing that remained terribly important – and quite rightly – was that we should still cast Scottish actors and not ask English actors to assume Scottish accents. That is a kind of house rule, even with the smaller parts, because people in Scotland do get very irritated if the accents are wrong.'

Peter said he insisted that authenticity was going to be the keynote for every element of the series. 'I was also very keen that it shouldn't become a "Scottish series" – it just happens to be set in Scotland. I wanted to get away from the cosiness of pipes and kilts, and all that sort of thing.'

How then, I asked, did Peter choose his quartet?

'It was a tall order in talking this through with everyone concerned. However, I chose David Rintoul for Finlay because he is the kind of "Everyman" actor I like. He doesn't come with any baggage. He was not *that* well known – or should I say, he wasn't that well known *then*. So, there could always be a bit of anonymity to his playing.

'There was no one else who could have played Dr Cameron and Janet, besides Ian and Annette. They are both very natural actors; Ian, if you let him, will go a bit wild, so all that energy has to be controlled, while Annette is straight down the middle. I looked for a long time before I auditioned Jason Flemyng for Dr Neil. In his case, we had to make an exception to our rule: although his parents are Scottish he was brought up in England. The offers then went to all of them and we held our breath.

'Ian hummed and hahed, and it seemed as if he might pull out, just as he had done from the original *Dr Finlay's Casebook*. [See Chapter Seven] So I worked very hard to keep him in the picture because we really felt we did not have anyone else to fall back on. When they all finally agreed, that was the first hurdle over. The second was people's prejudices, because in all our discussions there were those (understandably) with pre-conceived ideas of what the series is about.

The car passed another sign, marked to Tullibole Castle, and Peter elaborated on another tricky element in his pre-production plans.

'As producer, you have to stage-manage the ideas and come up with a vision that is your own and sell it to everyone – the writers, the actors, the designer,' he said. '*Doctor Finlay* is a format show, but in fact we can go down any road we want and do almost anything, within reason. It is a character-driven series, not necessarily a medical series. It is about these characters who live in a small Scottish town – they happen to be doctors and Janet happens to be the housekeeper. So it became a question of balance: putting a mix of medical stories in with the balance of the characters which then drove the whole pro-

duction along.'

The decision made by Robert Love and Bill Craig to set the series in the year 1946 was, Peter says, very clever. 'Because the first episode, "The Return", was Finlay returning from the war, you could also say it was the return of *Doctor Finlay*, the series.'

Because Peter Wolfes is so evidently an enthusiast for drama that engages the audience, he decided upon what he called a series of 'buzz words' for the production team. 'When I had my first discussion with the writers and directors, I banned certain words: "rural", "nostalgia" and "sentimentality" were three prime examples,' he recalled. 'I didn't want to rely on a sense of nostalgia or sentiment because period drama can become a cliché in itself: you're always allowing the period to dominate proceedings.

'I wanted to make a series that engaged the audience – I didn't just want them to sit there like . . .' (At this, Peter pulled a face resembling the classic 'couch potato', which prompted a surprised look from a lorry driver coming in the opposite direction.) 'We've got great characters, so I wanted stories that either make you laugh, or cry, or get angry – drama that emotionally involves you. I think we have succeeded and the trick now is to sustain it.'

For a while Peter drove on in silence and then, as we passed Kinross, I noticed the first sign for Auchtermuchty and decided this was a suitable moment to introduce the subject of the little town which had been chosen to represent Tannochbrae.

'The brief about the location was obviously partly financial,' Peter continued. 'It was to try and keep everything within an hour's drive of Glasgow because of the cost of overnight payments. This was a tall order because Glasgow and its environs have changed quite a bit in recent years. Any derelict property has been renovated if it's within driving distance of Glasgow because it's so desirable. So it has been quite a struggle to find suitable locations for the period. At one time, I had five location managers all out looking for places.

'But every TV production needs its bit of luck. I knew how Tannochbrae should look in my own mind, but the more we looked, the more I started doubting my own image because so many small Scottish towns just have a main road going through them, or else a big high street. I had the added worry that once you committed a series to a location and shot it, there is no reversing the decision. A series like this will take an option for five years on a place, if not longer, so it is a big commitment. All these decisions you make at the front end have got to be solid, for there can be no change.'

Another smile crossed Peter's face as he remembered the day almost two years earlier when he was driving along the self-same road we were now following. 'We were actually on our way to view another town a bit further along, called Newburgh,' he said. 'Just as we were passing through Auchtermuchty, we decided to pull off the main road. We turned up a small hill and into this market place with little shops and houses on all sides. I remember taking one look and saying, "Eureka". It had a sense of the period, with a magnificent town square. It was perfect: I knew that we had found our Tannochbrae.'

Peter had decided early on that the whole series was going to be shot on location;

Cast and crew at a read-through for the first series.

Auchtermuchty transformed: the design team had the challenging task of turning the 1990s town into 1940s Tannochbrae. In the process, all evidence of modern life had to be removed.

there would be no studio sets. Auchtermuchty had been found, the search continued for other suitable houses and buildings in the vicinity.

'We always find real houses and shoot inside them,' he explained. 'Of course this presents real problems for the team because a lot of the stories are set in small, working-class cottages with little rooms which are not easy to film in. But they do provide the right atmosphere. We often end up in the most unlikely places, filming in tiny spaces.'

One location Peter remembers particularly well from the first series was an old cottage hospital. Filming there was completed only just in the nick of time – and no thanks to some local criminals. 'The location manager was actually doing deals with thieves to stop them nicking the lead off the roof, so that we didn't have a building with no roof on it,' Peter recalls with a wry laugh. 'The day after we had finished shooting, the place was demolished to make way for new development.'

Why, if he had experienced all these problems, I asked Peter, did he not return to Callander, the little Perthshire town in the heart of the Trossachs, where the original BBC series was filmed?

'I never even considered it,' he said bluntly. 'There was no point. I told my production team that I didn't even want to go

(Left) *Setting up a scene for the first episode of the series and* (below) *the final shot on film.*

near the area. I had to let people know right from the start that we were not recreating the original series. So when viewers wrote in after the first episodes saying they were terribly disappointed that it was not like the original series, I replied that it was not supposed to be.

It was never our intention to recreate the original. It is amazing that people can get such rigid a view about something that isn't real.'

In fact, the reaction of some viewers has given Peter a special insight into the psyche of a part of his audience which he finds fascinating, if at times a little worrying. 'Doctor Finlay has annoyed quite a few people,' he explained. 'I have had letters saying quite vociferously that it is far too real! I found this reaction when I was working on *The Bill*, too. If you psychoanalyse these letters, you realize that there are a lot of very lonely people out there who cannot cope with life. It's as simple as that. The last thing they want is something that shows them someone who is also unable to cope. But what do you do? It's a real dilemma, since not everything in life can be rosy.

'There are undoubtedly a lot of very susceptible people out there,' he continued, developing this theme. 'However, as I have said before, I feel strongly that it is possible to make a good drama series without resorting to violence, bad language or sex. What I am after is good story-telling with good performances. I believe that if you engage the audience emotionally, they can actually be more upset by that, because they have to use their own imagination to fill in some of the details, rather than being shown something too graphic. But don't get me wrong, we have shown some quite strong situations in the series, and will use some more in the future.'

Then recalling another controversial area Peter added, 'I know we have been accused of taking the series into a kind of quasi-political arena, but I completely deny this. Medicine deals with the human condition, so you are bound to get involved with politics. For instance, some people accused me of using *Doctor Finlay* as a way of bashing the modern NHS, by showing how good it was when it was first set up. But this is not true. The same illnesses existed in 1846 as they did in 1946. In the Nineties, it's just that modern drugs and laser treatment give you more of a chance; but the same social conditions persist: abortion, rape and so on. The series does have an edge, but certainly not a political bias.

'I also made it clear that I didn't want to make a period-style *Casualty* – I wanted an accurate picture of life in 1946. And to make sure we get things right, we have our own medical adviser, Dr David Park, a practising GP in Lanarkshire. He has been invaluable for the scenes involving surgery in the mid-Forties, as well as putting us right about the kind of intuitive diagnosis (based on local gossip as much on the patient's symptoms) which was then the basis of general practice in rural areas such as Tannochbrae.'

As the signs for Auchtermuchty grew more frequent, Peter admitted to me that he had even considered changing the name of the town where the stories are set. 'I don't particularly like the name Tannochbrae,' he said. 'Every time you say it, it sounds a bit soft, even twee. But I decided to stay with it in the end.

'I was firm about the use of the surrounding countryside, though,' he continued, 'and right from the start, I went on what I called an "anti-Trossachs" drive. What I didn't want was chocolate-box imagery. I wanted the series to look good in terms of production values, of course, but I didn't want to get lulled into scenic quality at the expense of the drama, although you can't escape it altogether because it's all around you.

'I wanted stark, bleak locations that look interesting; and I particularly wanted to establish that Glasgow's not far away, to show that Tannochbrae is part of the wider world.'

Now that we were in the heart of the kind of Scottish countryside that AJ Cronin wrote about in many of his books, I asked Peter how familiar he was with the author's work.

'STE bought the rights to use the names of Cronin's characters,' he said, a strong note of emphasis punctuating his words. 'That was it. But I did study the two books that inspired the first series, *Adventures in Two Worlds* and

An intimate moment between David Rintoul and Margo Gunn (as Nurse Brenda Maitland) - and the sound man came too.

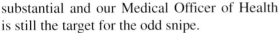

Adventures of a Black Bag. Early on, we decided to add a new, younger doctor to the practice, but to dispense with Dr Snoddie. He may have been popular in the Sixties, but he was too much of a stereotype for today. I wanted a character that would be more substantial and our Medical Officer of Health is still the target for the odd snipe.

'When I was in drama documentaries, we had a phrase: "to remain true to the spirit of a story". So with any story, we wanted it to show in essence the spirit that was behind the story rather than showing all the nuts and bolts, which is impossible anyway. I hope that in *Doctor Finlay* we have remained faithful to Cronin's spirit: i.e. we know that he was a socialist-minded GP, and we have made Finlay into a Labour supporter, if you like, without saying so. He cares for the conditions of his patients and is quite outspoken – but not to the point of being polemical. I would hope that if Cronin were to watch the series, he would think: "Yes, that has the right feel; it's what I had in mind."

'I am sure that at the time, *Dr Finlay's Casebook* was saying some pertinent things, within its own format, which were believable. But now we have so much more information and audiences are so much more sophisticated, we can cram a lot more information into fifty minutes.'

Peter's objective of bringing a greater sense of realism to the series has also been helped considerably not only by being made on location, but also by being shot on film instead of video. 'This enables you to get so much more detail into every scene,' he says. 'And this is not just a physical thing, but a mental process, too, because an actor has the freedom, through the use of the close-up, to do more that is *unspoken* rather than said. As a result, you can have two or three things going on at the same time. An actor can say one thing and give the impression of thinking another, which is not something that can be done comfortably in a TV studio because you get lost in the mechanics and all the other paraphernalia.

'Film gives you that ability to get more grainy,' he added. 'In fact, that's one of the things I think I've enjoyed most: the look of

Dr Finlay's Casebook:

CALLANDER: A TOWN OF MEMORIES

*I*T IS ONLY THE MEMORIES of *Dr Finlay's Casebook* that still live on today in Callander, the small Perthshire town at the junction of the rivers Teith and Lemy, which the BBC made familiar to millions of viewers as the first Tannochbrae. Once, thousands of visitors poured into the little burgh every year to look for Arden House, Mistress Niven's cottage and the Bard Street slums – not forgetting the Thornshaw Isolation Hospital – which had all taken on a reality of their own thanks to the series. But not any more.

Although Callander is still a holiday resort with an excellent golf course and offers fine trout and salmon fishing, only the ghosts of Dr Finlay, Dr Cameron and Janet haunt the locality, sustained by the recollections of the older residents who remember the halcyon days when their town was the most famous rural community on television.

The allure of the Trossachs all around this town of 1,800 people certainly remains as strong as ever, and Stirling District Council has done a good job in promoting it as an ideal starting point for touring the region and visiting the spectacular Loch Katrine away to the west. But accepting that their role as the mythical home of Dr Finlay has been supplanted, has not been easy for the local folk. Indeed, they were initially optimistic of a return to fame and fortune when Scottish Television announced they were to make the new *Doctor Finlay*, but this soon turned to disappointment at the subsequent, unequivocal statement that it would not be filmed in Callander.

There is no doubt that the coming of the BBC to Callander in the Sixties brought prosperity of a kind it had never experienced before, or since. Nowhere is this more dramatically illustrated than in the Crags Hotel, which was a favourite drinking place for the original cast and crew. The landlady, Billie Stewart, said recently:

'The series made us rich and busy for a short time. When *Finlay* was on the TV, and even for a few years afterwards, we used to get 3,000 people here each day. The Crown Hotel was even in the *Guinness Book of Records* for selling more meals in a day than anywhere else in Scotland. But that's all changed now. Some folk

(Above) *1920s Callander...*

call Callander 'dreich', meaning grim, and that's about right.'

The original property which featured as Arden House – Auchengower House – does still exist, and Dorothy McGregor, the owner for the past dozen years who now runs it as a guest house, was one of the first residents to be quoted in the press about her disappointment that the new Dr Finlay and his partners would never be returning there for a meal of beef or kippers, an afternoon cup of tea and a slice of walnut cake, or even a comforting whisky and cocoa at the end of another hard day. No matter what Scottish Television did, she told me, putting on a brave face, 'this will always be the BBC's Arden House and this town will always be Tannochbrae.'

Callander had been perfect for a Twenties serial recreating an atmosphere which has been described as 'quaint and very Scottish'; however, the demands for a saga now set in the post-war years were quite different. The times have changed, only the names remain the same.

...(below) *and how the town looks today.*

the series and our ability to let things run simultaneously to the main plot line,'

As we neared the outskirts of Auchtermuchty, a drop of rain suddenly bounced on to the car's windscreen, shortly followed by others. Although the rain developed into nothing more than a fine drizzle, the sight of it brought another wry smile of recollection to Peter's face.

'We have to fight the weather all the time in Scotland,' he said, as if sensing my question. 'Making a drama series like *Doctor Finlay* is rather like a military campaign: the planning is all important. We know how difficult the filming will be because you are always up against an ever-changing set of circumstances. The variables are infinite: the unexpected sounds of voices or bits of machinery starting up, the weather changing in the middle of a scene. We have to be flexible and ready to make sudden changes.

'We are constantly at the mercy of the elements here,' Peter repeated, as he switched on the car's windscreen-wipers. 'Last summer, it was like the Battle of the Somme. There was one location that was just so muddy. On the screen it looked very good, but trying to work in it was quite another matter. The rain has to be horizontal, though, for us to stop!'

Whatever the state of the weather, Peter believes that *Doctor Finlay* must always keep the viewer guessing as to what will happen next. In the first series, it was the question mark over whether Dr Cameron would leave the practice; while in the second it is the likelihood of Janet getting married. In his role as the producer, Peter has endeavoured to keep things 'bubbling along' in this way by using several quite different script writers. 'I am always on the look out for writers with something to say; sometimes even writers who are mavericks, so that you are never quite sure what you are going to get. I urge them all to

dig deeper into the characters because it is very easy for a series like this to become conventional.'

Peter then revealed how chance can also play a part in creating a successful element in a series. 'One of the things that came out of the first series was, in a sense, accidental,' he said, 'but will prove to be a big element running through the later episodes. It is the thought that if Janet marries the chemist, Angus Livingstone, then Dr Cameron rather regrets that he didn't ask her himself. There is this underlying feeling that they have known each other for a long time, and perhaps he has missed his opportunity. He is a bachelor, after all. Maybe Janet thinks the same, too; although they would probably say to each other: "That's ridiculous – a housekeeper and the master of the house!" But it's there, all the same.

'This all came about through the way Ian and Annette acted with each other. Ian is always after those kinds of moments as an actor – continually trying to push things – while Annette is always trying to push him back. It was really wonderful to watch, and gave the series a whole new dimension.'

As Peter finished talking, we arrived in Auchtermuchty. He made a sharp left turn across a small bridge, up a narrow street between rows of grey-stone houses, and turned left again into a market square. Although evening was beginning to fall, the effect could not have been more dramatic.

Indeed, for just an instant I thought we actually had travelled back almost fifty years in time. There was a pre-war bus stationary outside the shop of Thomas McGhee, newsagent, two Thirties cars side-parked in front of The Salvation Hotel, and several pushcarts and bales of hay around a cluster of empty wooden sheep pens beside the War Memorial, in the centre of the square.

But it was the modern film camera on

its little track of rails in the far corner of the square, surrounded by a group of men and women dressed in thick jackets against the encroaching cold of night, which belied the fact. That, and the lettering printed across the large window of the Union Bank of Scotland which stated it was the 'Tannochbrae Branch'. I had arrived at Doctor Finlay's patch, and would soon be meeting the people who had brought to life once again the most enduring of television's doctors.

Jason Flemyng and David Rintoul weather the muddy conditions on location.

Chapter Five

ON CALL WITH
THE DOCTOR

THE MORNING DAWNED BRIGHT and clear over the grey rooftops and narrow streets of Auchtermuchty. Although the time was not yet seven o'clock, there were already plenty of signs of activity in the market square and in the streets leading to the centre of the small community that for a week in August was being transformed into Tannochbrae.

Even at this hour, the door of Tannochbrae's The Salvation Hotel was open, the day's newspapers were in the rack outside Thom McGhee's newsagents shop, and there were stirrings of life behind the windows of the police station, 'Christine's' the fruiterers and, a little beyond the square, in the chemist's shop run by Alex Livingstone. A number of local people who had been hired for the day as extras were also out and about, hurrying to the make-up and wardrobe vehicles parked outside the square, while the mobile kitchen nearby, which is able to feed over a hundred people at a sitting – stars, extras, technicians, production team and all – was already busy serving up breakfast. At the far end of the square, Patrick Lau, the director of the episode about to be filmed,

Auchtermuchty becomes Tannochbrae for the start of another day's filming.

(Opposite) *A typical callsheet used during production of* Doctor Finlay, *detailing all the information relevant to that day's shooting.*

DATE: Tuesday, 24th August **DOCTOR FINLAY SERIES II**   **CALLSHEET NO: 43**

Producer: Peter Wolfes	**Production Office:**
Director: Patrick Lau	Forest Hills Hotel
	Tel: 0337 28318
LEAVE BASE: 0730	
ON SET: 0800	**LOCATION:**
Breakfast available from 0730	1. The Square
LUNCH: 1300	Auchtermuchty
WRAP ON SET: 1930 est	

SET	Sc No	SCR.DAY	I/E	D/N	Page	CAST
1. TANNOCHBRAE						
HIGH STREET	63	3	EXT	M	1/8	1.5.20.22
Janet & Rachel window shopping						26
HIGH STREET	63a	3	EXT	M	7/8	1.5.20.22
Rachel runs from Burns						26
SQUARE	63b	3	EXT	M	2/8	1.5.20.22
Burns & Stoddart watch Rachel						26
HIGH STREET	197	32	EXT	D	2 2/8	2.8
Hannah will have a cup of tea						
HIGH STREET	163pt	31	EXT	D	1/8	8.9.11
Berry kids walking through town						
HIGH STREET	232pt	33	EXT	D	4/8	2.8
Finlay passes Hannah						
HIGH STREET	163pt	31	EXT	D	1/8	8.9.11
Berry kids walking through town						
HIGH STREET	164	31	EXT	D	4/8	8.9.11
"Good morning, girls"						
HIGH STREET	232pt	33	EXT	D	4/8	2.8
Finlay passes Hannah						
					Total: 4 5/8	

ARTISTE	CHARACTER	P/UP	W/R	M/UP	L.UP	ON SET
26. JOE MULLANEY	P.C. Stoddart	0730	0745	0815	--	0830
20. FINLAY WELSH	Mr Burns	0750	0815	0825	--	0830
22. PHIL McCALL	Mr Strickland	0750	0815	0825	--	0830
1. ANNETTE CROSBIE	Janet	0740	0800	0815	--	0900
5. ANNE KRISTEN	Rachel Gant	0810	0830	0845	--	0900
8. GILLIAN REITH	Hannah Berry	1010	1030	1045	--	1130
2. DAVID RINTOUL	Dr Finlay	1040	1100	1115	--	1130
9. STEPHANIE ELLIOT	Miriam Berry	1210	1230	1250	--	1400
11. LISA ADAM	Sarah Berry	1210	1230	1250	--	1400

Crowd:		W/R - M/U				ON SET
32 x passersby (incl drivers)		0630				0815
7 x kids		0730				0815

Props:	Finlay's bag, Hannah's shopper (cont), Hannah's purse (cont), Hannah's shopping list, milk cart, Mrs Caldecot's milk jug, Berry children's bibles, Janet shopping bag, Rachel's string bag.
Action Vehicles:	Dr Finlay's car, coal lorry, hay cart (and dog), bus, Strickland's car and 2 x dressing vehicles on location for 0745
Camera:	2nd camera
Facilities:	Make-up + wardrobe vehicles heated, lit and ready by 0615 Artistes Green Room in Forest Hills Hotel, open and ready from 0730. Town Hall open and ready from 0630
Visitor to Set:	Peter Haining (writer of "On Call with Doctor Finlay").
Rushes viewing:	On wrap in Town Hall.
Chaperones:	Mrs Elliot and Mrs Adam on set

Willy Wands - Assistant Director

The crew set up for filming in the streets of Auchtermuchty.

was a triumph of the designer's art. So before shooting began, I decided to take a conducted tour of the whole area with the person who had been responsible for its total transformation, the production designer, Marius Van Der Werff.

Marius, a deceptively laid-back and cheerful man, has one of the most onerous yet least publicized jobs in television. In fact, he brings a formidable wealth of experience to this latest assignment, having worked on a whole range of productions from the much acclaimed BBC series, *Para Handy*, about a Clyde puffer and its loveable crew of eccentrics, to Scottish Television's recent success, *Taggart*.

and his assistant, Willy Wands, could be seen huddled together discussing camera positions with their crew. Close by, huge arc lamps were being hoisted into position to light the set.

The filming of the location scenes for *Doctor Finlay* which were taking place in the town, were the culmination of months of planning and weeks of refurbishing and redecoration on the site. Indeed, the area in which members of the unit were now hard at work, in order for filming to start at eight o'clock,

'It's essential with a series like *Doctor Finlay* that everything we show on camera is from the correct period,' he explained, as we strolled across the town square. 'My job is to find everything from suitable streets and houses right through to the wallpaper in individual rooms, and even the handles on doors. Believe you me, if we let something appear on television that wasn't around at the time, somebody out there will spot it and write in to complain.

'Discovering places still suitable for a series set in the Forties is the first problem,'

Marius went on. 'Not so long ago, rural Scotland was full of unspoiled properties, but now virtually everything has been updated. We have to spend months checking out possible locations and buildings, and then probably just as long renovating them so they look in period.'

All kinds of modern fixtures and fittings may have to be removed from a site before it can be used for filming. Traffic signs are the first to go, followed by white and yellow road lines which have to be covered by fake cobble-stones. Modern houses which may intrude into the background of a street scene similarly have to be disguised behind false walls, while telephone wires and television aerials are a constant headache.

'Virtually every house has a TV aerial,' said Marius, pointing up at a row of them on the roofs of the granite houses, along the top of the square. 'We have to take them down first thing every morning and then put them up again as soon as we finish shooting, at dusk. People can get a bit upset if they can't watch their favourite programmes, and we have to be up the ladders smartly whenever there's something like *Coronation Street* about to start.'

The biggest job of all is repainting buildings to give them the drab and austere look that typified so many properties in the immediate post-war years. Colourful reds and blues have to give way to browns and fading yellows on the fronts of the shops, while the walls of the larger buildings, such as the hotel and police station, need coats of grey to give them a suitably dingy appearance. Windows and doors often have to be changed or covered by imitations. Stains, dirt-streaks, cracks and even holes are all part of the production team's art.

Marius himself has to be the soul of discretion, compromise and understanding, to ensure that the people of Auchtermuchty

allow his team to make the necessary alterations to their homes; at the same time, assuring them that everything will be returned to normal after the crew have finished.

'We made a point of telling people right at the start that filming is disruptive,' he said. 'We have to close off the square to traffic without inconveniencing vehicles on the main road. We also circulated information to all householders in Auchtermuchty giving them details of our schedules and apologizing in advance for any disruption.

'There was even a printed circular which pointed out that while there would be pedestrian access to the areas we were filming in, residents were asked to avoid on-street parking there on the days we were shooting. Actually, the people here have been very good, most of them have just got on with their lives as usual.'

Marius then explained why these precautions were so necessary. 'There are lots of horror stories in television lore about film units leaving people in towns such as this with a very bitter taste in their mouths,' he told me. 'Unpaid bills, restoration work not carried out, and all kinds of damage to people's property and their feelings. Because we need to work here this year, come back again next year, and probably the year after, it's very important not to upset anyone. I won't say that everything has been perfect, but there have been no real problems so far.'

Even while Marius is supervizing this part of the production in Auchtermuchty, he is already thinking ahead. Other locations for scenes in later stories need to be scouted and, when found, the necessary arrangements made with the owners. He also has to be constantly on the look-out for a whole variety of props.

'When you have so many commercial and dramatic situations set in the Forties, there is a huge demand for everyday items from the

(Left) *The bright colours of modern Auchtermuchty had to be painted over to give buildings the grey and austere look typical of the period* (below).

period. Packets of tea and coffee, soap powders and cleaning fluids, boxes of breakfast cereals and jars of marmalade and jam, chocolate bars, sweets, crisps – the list is almost endless. And they've got to be genuine.'

Marius is quick to pay tribute to Robert Opie, 'shopping basket historian' and preserver of the disposable, whose remarkable collection of boxes and packets which once filled the homes of our parents and grandparents, has been a prime source of supply for the series. For it is primarily from this collection that he has filled the kitchen shelves and shop windows which appear in *Doctor Finlay*. Robert, the son of Peter and Iona Opie, the historians of children's lore and literature, began his collection over thirty years ago while he was living in Inverness, and now has a museum in Gloucester containing over 300,000 items which is claimed to be the largest storehouse of advertising and packaging material in the world.

'He has just about any kind of commercial container you can name from the Victorian period onwards,' Marius went on, 'which is remarkable when you consider that most bits of packaging are considered to be rubbish and thrown away once the contents have been used. Robert has saved everything he has bought, and added to these with stuff he has collected from all over the place. He's been invaluable to us.'

Just how invaluable, Marius demonstrated as we walked around Tannochbrae looking into the various shop windows. Decorative tin boxes of biscuits and sweets were very much in evidence, as were cardboard boxes of proprietary medicines such as 'Aspro' and 'Carter's Little Liver Pills'. Although all the packages of edibles I saw had obviously long been emptied, the crisp bags hanging in one window seemed full of goodies which

The production designers have to make sure that Tannochbrae's shop windows are full of authentic post-war commercial items.

Marius admitted were actually made from bits of plastic shaped to look like crisps.

The production designer also let me into the secret of the everyday use of the various buildings we passed. At the top of the square stood the impressive local branch of the Union Bank of Scotland, which for the rest of the year is the offices of the North East Fife District Council. The Salvation Hotel, just across the road, usually serves as the town's busy Forest Hills Hotel (and, indeed, was a centre of activity during the filming, as it was being used as the unit's production office) while Munro's the haberdasher's next door, with its display of 'Blue Lagoon Hose' and 'Sewing Susan' needles, is normally a carpet shop.

Immediately across the square from the hotel, the Auchtermuchty Town Hall and Library were now disguised as a police sta-

tion, while a false arch had been erected next to it to hide a pair of modern bungalows. Marius and I walked on past Helen Carmichael Gowns, which was, in fact, a ladies' outfitters, and then stepped through the doors of 'The Flying Dutchman'. I had expected to find myself in a pub, but instead discovered that I had, in reality, entered Jim McCrossan's Post Office and Stores.

The invented name intrigued me. Had it anything to do with Marius' nationality, I wondered? My guide's rueful grin as he bought a packet of cigarettes and a newspaper confirmed the story I had already heard from Peter Wolfes, that this had been the design

team's little joke on their boss!

We walked on, passing the well-stocked windows of Christine's the fruiterers (carrying on its normal function) and reached Thom McGhee's newsagent shop displaying copies of *The Tannochbrae Post & Advertiser* and – with a nice acknowledgement to the previous series – some issues of *The Callander Advertiser*, all hanging beside the door. The shop front, complete with bags of 'So Nice Potato Crisps' at 3d (old pence), 'Four Square Tobacco', and 'Crunchy Mints' at 6½d per quarter, proved to be just a façade occupying the front of a local resident's home.

A few yards further on we passed the chemist's shop embossed with the proprietor's name, A Livingstone, and an impressive, multi-coloured window display full of packets of 'Aspro', bottles of 'Dettol' and jars of 'Carter's Little Liver Pills'. This, too, proved to be part of a local home. Finally, we reached the flight of steps up to Tannochbrae Parish Church which was unmistakably Auchtermuchty's own little kirk.

A residential property is converted into Angus Livingstones' chemist shop, down to the last detail.

As Marius and I parted company, so that he could return to work on the morning's filming which was to be focused around the square, I continued my walk. I was keen to discover what other evidence there might be of the impact of the TV series on this little community, whose population numbers approximately 1,970 and whose heraldic motto is 'You Reap What You Sow', which has been tucked away undisturbed in the farmlands of Fife for centuries.

That the decision to film *Doctor Finlay* in 'Muchty has had an effect on the local people is not hard to see. Until the end of 1993 the town had a long-running 'Tannochbrae Tea Room' (a short walk from the square), and souvenir black and white tea towels designed by local artist Drew Bennett, together with car stickers proclaiming 'I Love Tannochbrae', are on sale in several of the shops. Conversations among the local inhabitants frequently turn to the filming, and there is plenty of typical Scots banter between those who are taking part as extras (at £55 per day) and those who are not.

'Are ye one of the film stars today?' a workman busy on a roof of a house calls out to a housewife walking towards the square.

'Fine breeks [trousers] y're wearing!' another passerby teases a friend going in the same direction, and obviously from his Forties demob suit on call for filming, 'even if they did come fra London!' (All the clothing for *Doctor Finlay* has, in fact, been supplied by a London costumier.)

But although the making of the series in the dour old granite town, which has been a royal borough since 1505, has certainly given it a higher profile, it was not altogether unknown beforehand. The name itself derives from a pictish settlement, Uachdarmuc, meaning 'high ground of the wild boar', and it is said to be located on one of Scotland's few extinct volcanoes. The town was also briefly notorious in 1818 for going bankrupt when some dishonest magistrates were thrown into jail and all the assets of the burgh sold off. A well-known local poem, *The Wife of Auchtermuchty*, is believed to have been written by King James V, while the name of the town has cropped up more than once in songs written by the local pop duo, twins Craig and Charlie Reid, known throughout Britain as The Proclaimers.

Perhaps a more significant event occurred in 1951 when King George VI and Queen Elizabeth drove past Auchtermuchty on their way to St Andrews, which is, of course, famous for its university (the oldest in Scotland, founded in 1411) and golf course. The royal couple's route was followed a little later by John Junor, the famous *Sunday Express* columnist (now of the *Mail on Sunday*) on his way to play golf at the Royal & Ancient. He stopped briefly in the town and went away struck by the way it had remained a bastion of traditional morality. A few weeks later, he wrote the first of many articles about Auchtermuchty. Of the town, Junor wrote: 'there is human decency and morality here, and the old standards act as a touchstone against modern life.' (It was also a place, he insisted, where homosexuality could not happen!)

Because of its curious name – which 'sounds like an old man clearing his throat', according to one rather unflattering description – many people outside Scotland believe that 'Muchty was just a figment of John Junor's mind, a place he had invented to bolster his censorious imagination. Indeed, it took the firm reproach of a famous resident of the town, Jimmy Shand, the accordionist whose band are a byword for Scottish country dance music, to assure everyone that it *did* exist.

ON CALL WITH DOCTOR FINLAY

Jimmy, who has now lived in 'Muchty for a total of thirty-six years, is regarded as one of its elder statesmen and perhaps *the* pre-eminent spokesman on matters concerning the town. He does, nevertheless, recall what a battle it was to convince people that the place was real. 'When I was travelling with the band,' he says, 'I used to ring home and ask for a reverse call to Auchtermuchty. Quite a few times the operator thought it was a joke.' The people of the town are, however, no joke, as Jimmy also adds quickly in his unmistakable Scots burr: 'Values depend on people – and here they are great homely people.'

The veteran musician, now in his eighties, confesses to having been a great fan of the original BBC series, and was one of the first to welcome the new *Doctor Finlay* to the town. But he also informed journalists that there was a certain undercurrent of feeling against filming on Sundays, the day traditionally set aside for attending the kirk. Curiously, too, he himself was involved in an incident of this kind shortly after the unit arrived to begin filming the first series in 1992. Unknown to anyone from STE, some preliminary filming had been scheduled for the very July day on which Jimmy's granddaughter was getting married. Producer Peter Wolfes recalls the event vividly. 'It was a big occasion: the wedding of the decade in Auchtermuchty. There was no contest; the filming had to be postponed. Jimmy won the day.'

Although the passage of time has, by and large, left the town unchanged in appearance since the early years of this century, there have been some social changes of late. The recession of the Nineties has no more passed Auchtermuchty by than anywhere else, and 100 people were made redundant a year ago when a local foundry was closed. There has also been a brush with drug-taking amongst the young (now thankfully stopped) and there

has not been an altogether universal acceptance of the town's first female minister.

But if the team from STE were looking for omens when they came to Auchtermuchty (other than the physical characteristics and atmosphere of the place) they were there to be found. On the Cupar Road which runs through the town, for instance, there is a Cameron House, while there are prominent local families named the Cruikshanks and the Simpsons. Nor was there a shortage of volunteers from among the local residents when the first calls for extras went out.

'Star-struck townsfolk turned up in their hundreds at the weekend, hoping to win a part in the new series *Doctor Finlay*,' the national daily, *The Scotsman*, reported on 29 June 1992. 'Movie-mania gripped 'Muchty when over 200 folk trooped to the church hall hoping for TV stardom. Some turned up for fun, others fancied the £55-a-day fee, and many were there simply to do their bit to support the community.'

Although very few of the extras had ever appeared in front of TV cameras before, there was one exception in John Watson, a retired drama teacher from nearby Kingskettle, who had actually done quite a lot of acting. John, aged sixty-one, had first appeared as an extra in *Z-Cars* more than twenty-five years ago, earning just £10. Then, later experience in rep at Lincoln, Bromley, Winnipeg, and at the Byre Theatre in St Andrews, had stood him in good stead for a return to television in *Doctor Finlay*. 'Who knows, this might be my big break at last?' John joked with pressmen.

Whether or not bit parts in the series will bring fame to any of Auchtermuchty's inhabitants is a matter for the future, but there is no doubt that the filming has turned the place into a tourist attraction now. In the past, most visitors to the area only glanced momentarily at 'Muchty as they sped by along the A91 to St Andrews and the Neuk of Fife's picturesque fishing villages.

'Those who came to visit us as a result of *Doctor Finlay* find the town is really not much different from what they've seen on the television,' Christine Fleming, the owner of the fruiterers, told me when I stopped in to buy some apples. 'The centre of 'Muchty is a listed area, you see, and we aren't allowed to change the shop fronts. So things look pretty much as they've always done. Mind you, seeing some of the houses painted in drab colours and watching horses pulling carts through the street does make you think of the days when there was no such thing as vandalism and you never had to lock your doors.

'We are certainly seeing more people coming here for a day out, taking pictures,' she added, bagging up my purchase. 'I don't suppose many people will travel up from the south of England, but the original series did a lot for Callander and it would be good if things got a bit busier here, though not too commercialized. I don't suppose it will make a lot of difference to my business. I can't see people carting tatties and fruit back to St Andrews, can you?'

Over in the Forest Hills Hotel (aka The Salvation Hotel), the proprietor, Ernst Van Beusekom, has reason to be grateful to STE for commandeering his building and is opti-

The production team had no problem in finding extras for the series, many of whom were local townspeople.

mistic about his business prospects for the future. 'I came here from Holland in 1965 and was given a wonderful welcome by the local people,' he explained. 'There's a tremendous community spirit and the people deserve a bit of a boost. I'm hoping it will bring in a flood of tourists and fill my rooms!'

Back out in the square, the chimes of the ancient clock on the tower of the town hall (aka the police station) were just striking eight o'clock when David Rintoul appeared, in order to begin filming the first scene of the day. And as he did so, I caught sight of Auchtermuchty's real doctor crossing the square towards a house marked with the number '17', where he would shortly begin his surgery at 8.30 am.

Dr David Adams, a handsome man in his early forties, who usually dresses in a bright Fair Isle sweater and tweed jacket, with clogs on his feet (ideal for muddy farm tracks) and little black bag in his hand, is the personification of a latter-day Dr Finlay. Indeed, it is an accolade he readily accepts, as I found out after I had introduced myself and explained my purpose in the town.

'Yes, I suppose my life is not that different from Finlay's,' he agreed, with a smile that suggested he had heard the comparison made before. 'I live right here among my patients and have a very warm relationship with them. I also care for them deeply. I have a housekeeper too, called Mary, who, just like Janet, keeps me in touch with village life.

'There are other similarities, too. I mean the superb quality of life we doctors have up here. People are friendly and honest and we have no real hassles. In fact, it seems that the spirit of Tannochbrae still manages to survive in people's minds and, almost, in reality.'

Unlike Finlay, however, Dr Adams shares his practice not with two partners, but three: another male colleague, Dr John Kerr, and two women, Dr Anne Ince and Dr Mary Brown. Between them, this quartet run three surgeries, one in Auchtermuchty and the others in the nearby villages of Falkland and Strathmiglio. In total they serve 6,200 patients in an area ten miles by six, in what is referred to as 'the Howe of Fife'. There is, though, no deputizing service and they have to do all their own night and weekend calls on a rota basis.

The filming of *Doctor Finlay* in the town has given Dr Adams a special interest in the life of a GP in this part of Scotland in the Forties, and the comparisons with today are not altogether favourable, he says.

In 1946, before the advent of the National Health Service, patients had to pay for their treatment and medicines. A home visit normally cost three shillings (15p) while the fee for a consultation in the surgery was half a crown (12½p), This, compared with bread at one shilling (5p), butter at one shilling and threepence, and one shilling and sixpence for a pint of beer. The cost of a prescription varied from a few pennies to several shillings, depending on the drugs. If the advice of a specialist was required, this could cost as much as £10 – more than the average weekly wage.

According to Dr Adams, many working men in the Forties contributed a few pennies each week to their firm's health scheme, while a lot of companies made donations to their local cottage hospitals so that their workers could get treatment. There were, however, no waiting lists then, mainly because few people could afford the cost of a consultant.

Although Dr Adams says there was no charge for entering hospital, people tended only to be admitted when they had an infectious disease and required isolation. Indeed, Auchtermuchty had its own fever hospital until it was closed down, shortly after the introduction of the NHS. It was replaced by the Perth Royal Infirmary, a voluntary hospital some twenty miles away. Dr Adams still sends patients there today, although it is now strictly 'across the border', in the Tayside Health Region. The only other alternative is a seventeen-mile journey to Victoria Hospital in Kirkcaldy, which is run by the local Fife Health Board.

The 'Muchty GP told me that surgery was undoubtedly primitive in the Forties, and it was not unusual for patients to die because there were no antibiotics available to fight infection. Babies were generally born at home, with a doctor usually charging £3 per delivery, while among those mothers who chose to go without medical services (or could not afford them), deaths of their infants as a result of complications were not unknown. The only ante-natal or postnatal care was provided by doctors, although most included it in their delivery fee.

It was not surprising, therefore, says Dr Adams, that his fictional counterpart, Dr Finlay, should have been enthusiastic about the introduction of free medicine for all. But Dr Adams now nurses a sense of foreboding about some of the reforms being proposed for the NHS; although, as yet, his fears that GPs might choose to become fundholders with their own budgets, buying health care for their patients, and that hospitals in the region could opt out to become self-governing trusts, have not yet materialized in Auchtermuchty.

'Thankfully, the NHS in our area doesn't seem to be so greatly underfunded as it is in many places,' he said, as we began to walk towards his surgery, 'and we have no trouble getting our patients into local hospitals. There are a few unacceptably long waits, but by and large we are quite satisfied.

'But we are worried that as the reforms are tightened, the health board will negotiate contracts to buy certain treatments from certain hospitals and this will reduce patient choice. We will no longer be able to send people where we, and they, want to go. It could cause difficulties because in some places around here, public transport is virtually non-existent.'

Dr Adams says that as a result of his calls over the years, all around Auchtermuchty, he can vouch for the fact that the countryside has actually changed little since the days of *Dr Finlay's Casebook*. The families he visits are little changed, many of them having lived in the same area for decades. He is also pleased that the social standing of the local GP has remained unchanged since the days of his fictional predecessor.

'The doctor here is on a par with the local minister, the bank manager and the school teacher,' he said, 'which has changed very little from Dr Finlay's time. Of course, that can put extra pressure on your social life, but it is still a great benefit to know your patients personally. Since we have a very stable population in Auchtermuchty, this means I know nine out of ten people who come into the surgery. I know their medical history, their problems, their families, and this allows me to be much more effective.' As I listened to these words, I couldn't help feeling they might almost have come straight from a piece of dialogue for *Doctor Finlay*, the star of which was now finishing rehearsing his scene in the square.

If Dr Adams has any regrets, it is that his job is more about preventative medicine and health promotion rather than treating the sick. It is still, though, a tough and demanding occupation. 'The work can be tiring,' he said, as we parted company at the doorway to number 17, 'especially when you are called out several times in the evening, and then have to

(Above) *The two young GPs, Finlay and Neil, meet for the first time.*

get out of bed a couple of times more during the night. It's not the best preparation for surgery at 8.30 am, but that's the price you have to pay. The demands may be enormous, but so is the job satisfaction.' (These were words I was to hear uncannily echoed when I came to talk to David Rintoul about *his* life and career.)

Before I left Dr Adams, he recommended that I talk to Dr Hugh Muir, his predecessor as GP in Auchtermuchty, who was now retired. Dr Muir had actually been practising in the district in the days when *Dr Finlay's Casebook* was being made and had been a fan of the original series. He would probably have some pertinent comparison to make between the two television adaptations, Dr Adams pointed out. And so it proved to be.

Hugh Muir, a jaunty and engaging man in his mid-eighties with a sharp Scots wit, still lives in the town where he was the local GP

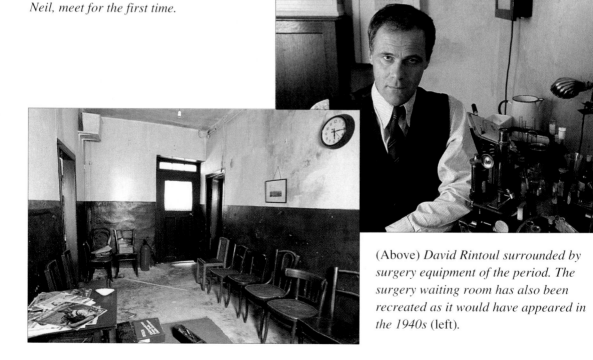

(Above) *David Rintoul surrounded by surgery equipment of the period. The surgery waiting room has also been recreated as it would have appeared in the 1940s* (left).

(Right) *Dr Finlay administers caring attention to some of the local children.*

(Below) *Cameron and Finlay treat Archie Henderson when a car accident threatens his life.*

from *Doctor Finlay's Casebook'.*

Dr Muir's list of patients ran into several thousands, most of whom had to pay, although there were a number of 'panel patients', he recalls, who were living below the poverty line and had their medical paid for by the local authorities. 'The most common illnesses were whooping cough, scarlet fever, diphtheria, rheumatic fever, measles, TB and pneumonia,' he said, effortlessly reeling off the list of ailments that had occupied his days, and nights, for half a century. 'There were frequent epidemics, I remember. Hospitals then were all voluntary and there were often fund-raising events to pay for their upkeep. But I don't remember any problems getting patients admitted.'

for over fifty years. He purchased the practice in 1944, and remembers the immediate post-war years very clearly. 'Aye, I ran the practice on my own in a cottage on the lower road that belonged to a Mrs Williamson,' he said. 'I used her dining room as a consulting room. Then I got married and moved into a house of my own and ran the surgery from there. The living room was the surgery and the hall was the waiting room. It was just like something

Like Finlay in the new series, Dr Muir

eagerly awaited the introduction of the NHS in 1948. 'But I think it is extremely doubtful whether it's any better now than when it was set up,' he said, reiterating the words of his successor, Dr Adams.

Unlike Dr Adams, however, he had the time to watch the filming of the first episodes of the new series, and was soon drawing comparisons with the BBC series. 'I was a great fan of *Dr Finlay* the first time around, and the making of the new series in Auchtermuchty brought back lots of happy memories,' he says. In fact, he was invited by a national newspaper to review the first episode of *Doctor Finlay*, and although immediately enthusiastic, the sharp-eyed medic also spotted one glaring error.

'The one thing wrong is Dr Neil's pushbike,' he wrote in the Sun on 5 March 1993. 'One gets the impression he is visiting his patients on a pushbike, but in 1945 I was driving my sixth car. There is no doctor in the country who possibly cover his patch on a pushbike. It doesn't spoil the film, but from the point of view of historical accuracy, it is wrong.'

Reading these remarks, I could hear Marius Van Der Werff's voice once again telling me that someone, somewhere, would always spot a mistake. Overall, however, Dr Muir thought the new series was excellent. 'They have portrayed the sort of doctor-patient relationship that was so important in our day, and it also gives the doctor the kind of prestige which he had in our time.'

Turning to the various characters, Dr Muir delivered his verdict: 'I would say this Dr Finlay is a lot better than the last one. David Rintoul is excellent. I always felt Bill Simpson was a bit harsh in his role as Dr Finlay, but David is not quite as abrasive and a lot more pleasant.'

He also had rave reviews for Ian Bannen as Dr Cameron and Annette Crosbie as Janet. 'I certainly didn't envy Annette Crosbie's task,' he wrote. 'I thought Janet was the mainstay of the series during the Sixties and she was someone you could really identify with. Barbara Mullen was simply superb in the role. But I don't think I can pay Annette any better compliment than by saying she was almost as good as Barbara. They are quite different, but it didn't detract from my enjoyment of the programme whatsoever.'

Dr Muir was also impressed by the storyline which involved Dr Finlay buying his share of the practice from Dr Cameron, 'for that's how it would happen in those days,' he added.

When I later returned to the market square in Auchtermuchty, the sun was already high in the sky, appearing occasionally from behind banks of cloud, although they seemed not threatening enough for rain. Filming was going on in the street, and a number of extras costumed in Forties suits and dresses were being rehearsed.

There were several men on bicycles with a couple more pushing carts, a flurry of small boys in caps, long shorts and knee socks, and a line of women obviously on their way to do their shopping. I was struck by the strong, weathered, typically Scottish faces of all these people, each one adding to the character and authenticity of the series. As the final finishing touches, a number of milk churns, some bales of straw, and a few piles of horse droppings had been laid carefully on one side of the street. As yet, there was no sign of a horse.

This attention to detail was equally evident when the film crew prepared to begin shooting. Just before 'action' was called, a member of the production crew shouted through his two-way radio to one of the assistants. He had spotted a red and white traffic cone in front of one of the vintage cars parked at the far end of the square.

'There's a cone up your end!' he hissed, urgently.

The bawdy laughter which echoed across the square was instantaneous and good-hearted, typical of the closeness of the unit and the spirit of teamwork which as become a hallmark of the production of *Doctor Finlay*.

As the offending cone was removed and the laughter subsided, Patrick Lau indicated again that he was ready to start filming. This, I decided, was an appropriate moment to leave. I was now keen to see the most famous house in the Tannochbrae legend, and to talk to the four residents who are the stars of the series.

Although meeting the quartet who have both individually and collectively contributed to the success of the programme proved no problem, Arden House was quite another matter. According to the scripts, the house-cum-doctor's surgery is located a bit further along the road from the chemist's shop, just outside the range of the camera.

In fact, like Tannochbrae itself, this proved to be another illusion. For Arden House is actually over fifty miles from Auchtermuchty, no more than a twenty-minute

Evoking the quiet streets of 1940s Tannochbrae.

Chapter Six

LIFE IN
ARDEN HOUSE

*A*RDEN HOUSE, the home of Tannoch-brae's trio of doctors and their indefatigable house-keeper, is an unremarkable building when glimpsed behind bushes from the end of a dirt road. A two-storey, whitewashed house with a steeply sloping roof and tall sash windows, it is not that different from many other buildings in the surrounding farming countryside full of corn-fields and grazing cattle. It is just the location of the property which at first strikes the visitor as rather curious.

To find this key house in the *Doctor Finlay* legend does not require a lengthy drive into the Scottish countryside, as might at first seem the case; it is, instead, just over ten miles from the centre of Glasgow, in the little town of Houston, in Renfrewshire. The drive from the city, via Govan and Paisley, takes the visitor from the hubbub of Glasgow into picturesque agricultural land where the towns have names like 'Bridge of Weir', 'Ranfurly' and, with echoes of another popular independent television series, 'Brookfield'.

It is a journey that also traces the flight

Arden House at twilight.

path of aircraft from Glasgow Airport; and the curious situation now occurs that passenger jets which were not yet even invented, let alone flying at that time, frequently pass over the property which is locked by design into the years following the end of the Second World War. But although these flights are

(Opposite) *The inhabitants of Arden House.*

occasionally seen and heard when the *Doctor Finlay* team are filming in Houston – and a few scenes have had to be reshot because of extraneous noise – there have been no serious setbacks to the schedule, Peter Wolfes told me.

Why, though, pick a building even approaching the vicinity of a major international airport?

'Once again, it was a question of finding somewhere within range of Glasgow that had the right period look,' the producer explained. 'I also wanted to find a real property for Arden House so that we could turn it into our own film lot. As was the case with Auchtermuchty, it meant a lot of location scouting, but once we had spotted the building, we knew it was right. Of course we were aware of the airport, but it was such a perfect location, it was worth it. And as I have already said, coping with noise and being flexible has been a part of our operation since the beginning.

'As for the appearance of the actual house, we had already decided that Dr Cameron had been living on his own while Dr Finlay was away at the war, so we felt that it should have a ramshackle appearance. The cost of hiring somewhere and deliberately making it look neglected would have been prohibitive, so we looked for something that was already in a state of disrepair.'

The property that the production team settled on was, in fact, a farmhouse on the outskirts of Houston which had been unused for years. STE leased it from the local laird, and the carpenters and painters moved in to tailor it to the needs of the period

The empty farmhouse (above) *eventually used for Arden House had its interior transformed for the series* (left).

(Right) *Dr Finlay's room after the design team had finished work on it, and the new kitchen for Arden House* (below).

finally decided to take it home each night for safety. An authentic 1940s post-box on a telegraph pole in front of Arden House was the object of another souvenir hunter. Apparently, a prolonged attempt was made one night to steal this, by a thief who tried to jemmy the steel bolts holding the box to the pole.

and the requirements of filming.

Remote though the 'new' Arden House is, and as secret as the team have tried to keep the location, sightseers have sometimes driven out from Glasgow and other surrounding areas to take a look at the farmhouse and try to get a glimpse of the stars at work. Worse still, some even began trying to steal souvenirs from the site as soon as shooting was finished for the day.

Among the valuable props outside the house which people tried to remove, was the brass surgery name-plate beside the front door. Several attempts were made to wrench it from the wall, and to save the cost of an expensive replacement, one of the production crew

'They almost got away with both of these items,' Peter Wolfes said, 'and after the attempt on the post-box, which is a genuine article from the period and irreplaceable, we felt something needed to be done. So we now have a round-the-clock guard on the site while we are filming there. I know fans of any series are always keen to see where it is made, and it's hard to discourage them. But we have appealed to people not to try to take bits of the location home with them.'

Since Peter's public appeal, there have been no incidents at Houston, but the team are under no illusions that the longer the series continues, the more a focus of attention it will become.

For the stars of the series, however, the location of Arden House has been more of an advantage than a problem, allowing them all to return to Glasgow at the end of a day's shooting.

'When you've been working in the open all day, in pouring rain, to get back at night to a warm bath and a hot meal in your hotel is a real joy,' David Rintoul, the new Dr Finlay, told me with a rueful smile of remembrance when we met. Hours of waiting for a scene to be shot on a bleak winter's day are one of the other, less glamorous sides of an actor's life.

David has now filmed his second series as the young Tannochbrae doctor, John Finlay, and has already made the character very much his own and quite different from his predecessor, Bill Simpson. A tall, handsome man, who looks every inch a country doctor when he is dressed in the brown tweed suit and stout brogues of the part, David is unassuming, friendly and refreshingly direct. He has a very clear vision about both the character and how to play him.

'I decided not to study the original series before I began filming,' he said, 'though obviously I remember it as a teenager in the Sixties because it was required viewing on Sunday evenings. I didn't want Bill Simpson's Finlay to inhibit my performance. He did a splendid job, but I can only play the doctor *my* way.'

David Rintoul as Dr John Finlay.

David believes that the reintroduction of Dr Finlay to viewers after he had served in the Royal Army Medical Corps in the war, was ideal for him as an actor. 'By starting as a soldier, I had an excellent opportunity to get inside the part. Finlay has just tasted the bitter fruits of war and is a changed man when he returns to Tannochbrae. He's been hardened by his experiences and, naturally, he's more cynical than before. He is also returning to a changed world. Scotland is emerging from the trauma of the war, and the role of medicine in the community is becoming an important issue, with free treatment and the National Health Service on the horizon. In fact, it is a fascinating era altogether, with lots of scope for controversy.'

Among the first scenes David shot for the series was the spectacular opening sequence in a German military hospital in Berlin, in 1946. 'I'll never forget that,' he reminisced. 'It was quite extraordinary. The set builders had totally transformed this partly-disused hospital complex, Woodilee Psychiatric Hospital at Lenzie, just outside Glasgow. There were over a hundred extras playing the parts of soldiers, dozens of military vehicles and a huge scaffolding tower: all for one shot. I was actually up on that scaffolding tower looking at it all, and I can tell you, the atmosphere was electric. It was some introduction to the part!'

David, who is forty-five, was born David Wilson in Aberdeen. (He changed his name to Rintoul – his mother's maiden name – when he joined Equity.) He came to his latest role, he says, with a number of striking advantages. 'I've been very struck by the similarities between Finlay's character and my own,' he says. 'My family, for example, came from farming stock, as Finlay is supposed to have done. My father, Dr Leslie Wilson, who's now retired, was a geriatrician for Aberdeen and also the visiting general physician for Orkney and Shetland; he served in Burma as a major in the Royal Army Medical Corps during the Second World War – also like Finlay. And I mustn't forget that my late uncle was also an anaesthetist.

'My father actually graduated from Aberdeen University in 1941 and returned from the war in 1946. He also told me that there was a great deal of resistance to the National Health Service then, especially from the hospital consultants. Aneurin Bevan, then Health Minister, said something like, "I've stuffed their mouths with gold". He just paid them a very good whack and they went along with it.

'I think it caused a big improvement in

A scene of the Berlin army hospital from the opening episode of the series.

the relationship between doctor and patient because people were much more inclined to go to their doctor. Indeed, the first thing that happened was that doctors' surgeries were absolutely mobbed and people would come in for anything and everything. It took quite a while for that to settle down.'

David says that throughout the filming he has been able to discuss the part of Finlay with his father, which has proved extremely useful. 'We have had a medical adviser on the set, but I still ring my Dad constantly to ask his advice, even on simple things like how to sound a patient's chest. He also helped out a lot with some of the trickier medical pronunciations. I even spent ages poring over old family photographs of him to get a feel for the period. Both of my parents, who still live in Cults on the outskirts of Aberdeen, were thrilled when I became a doctor – if only a fictitious one!'

Why, then, coming from such a background, didn't David actually follow a career in medicine?

'Medicine seemed too much like hard work,' he smiled. 'It's a hundred percent or nothing and I fancied acting. Dad had done a bit of student drama and my maternal grandmother was a good amateur actress. I got my first taste of acting at primary school and I used to write, direct and act in plays. Later, I joined The Longacre Players, who were part of the Aberdeen Children's Theatre, and I just got bitten by the bug completely.

'In fact, I very nearly appeared in the original *Dr Finlay's Casebook*. I had a couple of small parts in the TV series, *This Man Craig*, with John Cairney, about a Glasgow schoolteacher. This was being made in Glasgow at the same time as *Dr Finlay*, and both producers used kids from the Glasgow Drama College. When they had used all the kids in Glasgow, they started looking further afield to Aberdeen for some new faces. I auditioned for the part of a guitar-playing Sixties rebel, but nothing came of it.'

Instead, David went to Edinburgh University in 1966, where instead of drama he took a 'rag bag' degree in English and Philosophy. 'Edinburgh was such a melting pot for drama then,' he recalls, 'and there was a whole crowd of us, now in the business, who went through the late Sixties together. There were some marvellous talents: Sharman Macdonald, who went on to write *When I Was A Girl I Used To Scream And Shout!*, Tim Piggott-Smith, and my great mate, Ian Charleson, the star of *Chariots of Fire*, who died so tragically of AIDS just as I was getting my break in *Finlay*.

'It was the most shocking thing that has ever happened to me,' David digressed for a moment, in a voice little above a whisper. 'We were very, very close for twenty-odd years and even shared a flat together for months on end. He was the closest person to me outside my family. When I found out he had AIDS, I felt ghastly. But I admired his bravery so much; he handled it with dignity to the end, even playing Hamlet at the National Theatre, when he was thin and very weak and had a sinus condition. When he died, his parents decided to say he had AIDS and I think that helped to break the taboo of the disease in some way. I still miss him dreadfully: he's left an ongoing emptiness in my life.'

David was silent for a minute before returning to the details of his career. 'Anyhow, the Swinging Sixties were marvellous and we were into everything. I directed six plays and acted in about thirty in three years. They were manic times! After that, I went to RADA and then started working as acting stage-manager at Worthing, also playing the odd scene. My lucky break came when Pharic McLaren, a producer at BBC Scotland, was putting on an adaptation of Robert Louis Stevenson's *Weir of Hermiston*. He had apparently been looking for someone to play the young hero for some time, and I happened to turn up at the right moment. He cast me opposite Tom Fleming and it was a wonderful part, and a very lucky break for me.'

The exposure he received in this series led to a lot more television work in Scotland: mostly period dramas, David recalls. By way of contrast, he also worked in the theatre with what he describes as a shifting group of actors and writers (including David Hare and Bill Gaskill) in which the authors and the performers co-operated in producing contemporary radical plays.

When he reached his thirties, David changed the direction of his career yet again by taking on a number of classical roles, including Mr Darcy in the 1980 BBC version of *Pride and Prejudice*, before joining the Royal Shakespeare Company. He made a brief appearance in the movie, *The Legend of the Werewolf*, starring Peter Cushing, in which he played the lycanthrope, and then a more substantial appearance as the evil Dick, one of the villainous Mallens in the TV version of Catherine Cookson's famous novel of the same name. His casting as Dr Finlay now he is in his forties, has marked yet another change of direction.

David clearly remembers the days which transformed him from a journeyman professional actor who was rarely out of work, into a household name. My reaction to being asked to play Finlay surprised even me,' he said. 'The series had been mooted for some time and, of course, I had heard about it. Various names were being mentioned for Finlay, so I didn't really give it much thought. Then the day before I was due to go off to Sicily to do this rather peculiar job – a Beckett monologue for an Italian company, as part of a

huge drama festival – I had a phone call from my agent. He is normally a very cool sort of customer, but behaved in this rather atypical, excitable way and said I was being considered for Dr Finlay. Would I go and have a chat with Peter Wolfes? Well, we had a chat and that was that.

'Anyway, a couple of days later, I was rehearsing the Beckett at a place called Erice, which is a beautiful walled town on the north-west coast of Sicily, when I got this message, "Phone your agent". So I found a phone in one of those tiny tobacco kiosks and in that inept setting I was told I had got the job.

'I didn't hesitate for a moment: my immediate reaction was, "Yes, I want to do it." It was *so* immediate, I surprised myself. I had always thought that if something like this ever did come up – a part with which you could become terribly identified – it would give me a lot of thought. I decided that if I was going to do television, then I should do *good* television. And that is certainly the case with Doctor Finlay: lots of very good people and excellent scripts.'

David actually met his predecessor, Bill Simpson, as well as Andrew Cruikshank during his working life. 'I only met Bill a couple of times,' he says. 'But I worked with Andrew twice, the second time at the Edinburgh Festival when I was assistant director. Andrew must have been about eighty, but he was playing this corrupt bishop with enormous energy. He was a very generous man and did a lot of work for the Festival Fringe, for whom he was the chairman.'

I asked David if he was worried about the fact that life had not treated Bill Simpson very well after he had played Finlay, so identified had he become with the role.

'Of course, I don't want to tempt fate, but at the moment I'm very happy playing the part,' he said. 'We only work on Finlay for six

Dr Cameron receives the benefits of Finlay's bedside manner.

months of the year, which gives me plenty of chances for other things. I don't want to fall into the same trap, but who knows what will happen in this business?'

I then asked him how he viewed the character of Dr Finlay.

'I think he is quite a complex man. He was written fairly sternly in the first series, and I think I may have slightly overplayed the sternness and the held-in quality of the man. He was certainly in a bit of a churned-up state to begin with, but in the second series I have lightened him up without losing gravitas.

'There are all sorts of conflicts within him. I think he genuinely wants to be a GP and is quite happy to be one. He knows he has given up that other side of medicine: he is the kind of doctor who likes working with people rather than working just theoretically. He does have a sense of humour; it is quite dry, which is very Scottish.

'He also has very strong opinions and he's certainly got a short fuse. I hope he's not self-satisfied. He has political beliefs, too, and believes passionately in 'social' medicine and the setting up of the NHS.'

If David has had a problem with Finlay it is escaping form the image of him created by Bill Simpson. 'In the case of television series like *Sherlock Holmes* and *Poirot*, the characters are very well-defined in the original books. But Finlay is different. He was very well-defined by Bill Simpson's performance. People think of Dr Finlay *as* Bill Simpson. In a way, *because* there are no Dr Finlay books – apart from the two collections of short stories – the exercise for me was never, could never be, one of imitating Bill. In fact, I haven't got the hair for it! Seriously though, it is actually quite freeing: Finlay is a bit of a loose garment, you can wear him how you like.'

David prepares very methodically for every scene, writing out a copy of each day's script in long-hand. 'Actually using a pen and copying out every word helps me to visualize the sentences on the page,' he says. He much prefers location work to the studios ('it has an atmosphere all of its own') and gets on well with his co-stars.

'We are a good team,' he says simply. 'I've admired Ian for years and he is fascinating to work with. Annette is very good and spikey. I've actually worked with her twice before: once on TV in *The Member for Chelsea* and also on the stage, in Pirandot's *The Trojan War Will Not Take Place*, directed by Harold Pinter. She played my mother! Jason Flemyng is a bright young talent and a good lad.'

There have, of course, been many gaffes during the filming of *Doctor Finlay* which will never find their way on to the screen. Missed cues, props going haywire, actors dissolving into helpless laughter: David has experienced them all and, like his colleagues, taken them in good humour, even when members of the production team have chosen to screen these out-takes at the end of a particular period of filming for the amusement of the whole company. However, only one error on screen particularly sticks in David's mind:

'We had this opening sequence in which a baby had to be given some medicine,' he recalls. 'Well, everything went smoothly; the mixture was poured from the bottle and carefully spooned into the child's mouth. It wasn't until afterwards we learned that the bottle from which the medicine had been poured was only ever used for *poison*! Quite a few people wrote in about that.'

He also does his homework into medical practice very carefully and takes an increasing interest in the state of the profession in the Nineties, which he talks about with much of the insight of a real GP.

'I would say that the NHS is in a fairly sound state, although there are some areas that need treatment. Compared to the late 1920s, when the original *Dr Finlay's Casebook* was set. I think that patients today do get a better deal. There may not be so much of the cosy family doctor/patient relationship as exemplified by the old Dr Cameron, and to some extent by the impetuous young Dr Finlay, but I am sure that a lot of it still exists, particularly in the country

Dr Finlay with former fiancée Nurse Brenda Maitland – the pressures of war-time separation eventually caused their relationship to founder.

BILL SIMPSON AS THE ORIGINAL DR FINLAY

*I*N MOST ACCOUNTS of the beginnings of *Dr Finlay's Casebook*, Bill Simpson is described as having been plucked from his desk as a young newsreader at Scottish Television, to play the lead in the series and then become a star overnight. In reality, he had worked hard to become an actor at college and in repertory theatre, while his life had also, in some respects, been similar to the part he was cast to play.

Bill was born in 1932 in Dunure, a small village in Ayrshire, but spent his youth working on his grandfather's farm, 'in the region near Glasgow where Tannochbrae is set', he told me many years later when he was living in the Oxfordshire village of Ashton Upthorpe. (His house, called 'Old Pyles', had, incidentally, become known locally as 'Dr Finlay's Old Pyles'.)

'There was quite a lot of Dr Finlay in me,' he said. 'I came into a professional life from a background in farming, and so did he. I'm also a pretty impulsive man, like Finlay. He was someone I could relate to in his moods, too. Like me, he had great highs and also times of total anxiety. But I never found the medical side easy to handle. I was always surprised when people approached me; I expected them to want an autograph and instead they would ask me to diagnose some illness they said they had!'

Bill believed that luck played an important part in landing him the role of the young GP, whose full name in the original *Casebook* was Alan Finlay. 'I was the right person in the right place at the right time,' he said. 'I never expected to be a great star like Sean Connery, but I reckoned I could mix what talents I had into the right part – and that happened to be Dr Finlay. I was pretty apprehensive when we started making the series, and for a bit, I comforted myself with the thought that it was only scheduled for six episodes. But Andrew and Barbara were such professionals and got me through. After that, it just went from strength to strength. I couldn't have been happier for most of the time.'

Bill always looked forward to the opportunities of returning to Scotland for location work, and revealed to me that some of the earliest scenes outside the London studios were not actually shot in Callander at all. 'I remember very clearly that our first location shoot was at a place called Kilbarchan in Renfrewshire, which is just outside Glasgow,' he said. 'It rained most of the day and I spent a lot of the time fretting. Not long after that, the location was switched to Callander which, of course, has since become famous as the site of Arden House.' It is an even more curious fact – and a remarkable coincidence into the bargain – that STE should have also chosen for the updated series a locality less than two miles from Kilbarchan for their Arden House, at Houston in Renfrewshire.

Bill played the young GP Alan Finlay with passion and conviction, but also with a sense of the vulnerability of the young and inexperienced. His interplay with Andrew Cruikshank's older and worldly-wise Dr Cameron and Barbara Mullen's kindly but shrewd housekeeper, Janet, who could silence them both with a withering glance, was the foundation upon which the series built its enormous appeal. It had a greater impact on the public than almost any of its contemporaries, and Bill himself became a genuine doctor in many people's eyes. He was also for several years voted the nation's 'Number One Heart-Throb' and received thousands of fan letters every week. According to one report, even the Queen was a regular Sunday evening watcher of the series and once invited Bill for drinks aboard the royal yacht, *Britannia*.

The strains of working on the series (for which Bill was initially paid the then princely sum of £70 per episode) first took a toll on his marriage and then on his health. He had married actress Mary Miller at a little church beside the Lake of Menteith Hotel in 'Tannochbrae' territory, but even such an idyllic start could not prevent the union faltering. Then, when he was thirty-four, he suffered a mild heart attack. Fortunately, he was able to return to work within a few weeks without any apparent ill-effects.

In 1969, the sultry brunette Tracy Reed, the actress stepdaughter of the late film director Sir Carol Reed, was introduced into *Dr Finlay's Casebook* as the doctor's cool temptress. Bill fell in love with her both on screen and off, and the couple were eventually married in 1974. Despite having two daughters, Kelly and Katie, this marriage also ended in acrimony and divorce in 1982.

Sadly, when *Dr Finlay* was finally taken off the air, Bill Simpson found it hard to top his achievement. He continued in an adaptation of the *Casebook* on BBC radio until 1978, but with it came virtually the end of his career as a top actor. He did star in a West End musical, *Romance*, which closed after five days, and then attempted to recapture some of the magic of Finlay by playing a veterinary surgeon in a BBC series, *The McKinnons*, but this too was doomed to failure. 'It really didn't have a chance,' Bill said, in a rare philosophical moment. 'At the same time, the BBC had already commissioned the James Herriot series. It was a case of two different departments within the same organization working independently of each other.'

With some of his earnings from the *Casebook*, Bill had bought a house in Spain and a cottage in Scotland, not far from the location of his greatest triumph. But he became increasingly more depressed as the job opportunities grew fewer and fewer, and his resources dwindled.

'*Dr Finlay* made me and I'm not ungrateful,' he said to me when we talked in the winter of 1984. 'He is still remembered wherever I go by an awful lot of people and I am still recognized. But it was also a terrific strain and a big relief when it ended. I still love acting and as long as I can remember the lines and don't fall over the furniture, I'd like to go on until I drop.' These were to prove sadly prophetic words. A year later, he told another journalist: 'It all came to a head when *Dr Finlay* dried up for good, my other work collapsed, and I ended up broke.'

His last days were a tragic mixture of declining health and stories of drinking problems and money disputes with his ex-wife which invariably found their way into the tabloid press.

Bill died on 21 December 1986, four weeks after entering Ballockmyle Hospital at Mauchline, near Glasgow. This generated headlines such as 'Dr Finlay Loses His Fight For Life' but created a mystery that would have been worthy of an episode of the *Casebook* itself. For after his death had been announced, a hospital spokesman added: 'In accordance with his wishes, we are giving no information as to what he was suffering from. There is absolutely no question of him having AIDS, nor had he cancer or heart disease. There is unlikely to be a post mortem since we know what was wrong with him, as he did himself.'

It was a sad epitaph for a man who had given such pleasure to millions of television viewers for over a decade; a fact that was echoed by Jean Rook in her *Daily Express* column, two days before Christmas:

'I can't believe that nice young doctor is dead. Yes, I do know I'm twenty years out of date. And that actor Bill Simpson, whose career died when they closed Dr Finlay's Casebook, *was a white-haired fifty-four with a drink-related problem. But as owner of that fallen, once household face, later passed over, but never bitter, said: "When the series finally ended, one felt slightly disappointed, but Dr Finlay is still remembered by an awful lot of people." He is. As if it were yesterday.'*

Finlay confronts John Moore (Eoin McCarthy) about his father, on the hillsides of Tannochbrae.

today in private medicine with those of the years just prior to the introduction of the NHS. 'It must have varied from person to person. The financial arrangements were actually very strange and difficult to organize. Very often, a small town doctor like Dr Finlay would do a sort of presumptive means test. He would guess at what a person could afford.

practices.'

The main difference between the embryo NHS in which Dr Finlay operates and that of today, he believes, is that the whole concept of a public health service as the main source of medicine is being questioned. 'Personally, I wouldn't like to see us have the same kind of set-up as America. I think we can learn from other people's mistakes. There, private medicine is the main provider and the public medical service is the safety net. I was brought up to believe that the main provider was public medicine and that was good enough. Private medicine was more or less marginalized. If you particularly wanted a private room and smoked salmon for lunch and could afford it, you went private. I think private medicine has been creeping in gradually over the past few years and it's an unfortunate trend. I would like to see more emphasis on public medicine, on building the NHS back up again.'

David then compared the charges levied

'In fact, the question has already been put in the series: "Do you think they're going to be able to afford five shillings?" one of the doctors says. "Well, maybe charge them three bob . . ." That was quite a responsibility to put on the physician.'

Evidently, David Rintoul has thought long and hard about his role, which explains the depth of his characterization and why it has so captivated viewers. How, though, does he relax when he puts away his stethoscope and little black bag?

'Well, I live in Fulham with my girl-friend, Vivien Heilbron, who is also an actress and who has appeared in *Sunset Song* as well as *Brookside* and *Taggart*. We are both fairly keyed-up people who can get quite fiery. But we both share a similar sense of humour and enjoy going out to dinner or the theatre. We especially like to soak up the sun to unwind.'

David Rintoul waits for 'Action!' to be called during a scene in the Salvation Army hall.

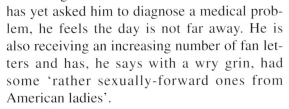

Whether appearing in public in the future will be quite so easy for David is now an issue he is having to face. He gets recognized in the street, but finds that people are remarkably discreet, even shy. There are also the 'I know the face, but can't place it' glances, and though no one has yet asked him to diagnose a medical problem, he feels the day is not far away. He is also receiving an increasing number of fan letters and has, he says with a wry grin, had some 'rather sexually-forward ones from American ladies'.

By and large, however, people have been very kind, he says, especially in Scotland. He has repaid this kindness by making personal appearances and opening local fêtes. He still smiles about the Doune & Dunblane Agricultural Show where he was invited to judge the children's pet show and present the prizes. During the course of the day, he was introduced to the two local doctors, one male and one female. Both were called Dr Finlay.

Recently, when David and Vivien took their usual break from work in Greece (they've been going to the same spot for ten years, and always on a package holiday) he had the first signs that his celebrity might be about to change dramatically.

'We did wonder if it was wise. But for most of the time, we were able to do everything we wanted. Then one night as we were just leaving a restaurant, had gone around the corner and were out of sight of the tables, we heard a voice: "Good night, Dr Finlay," it said, and was followed by a giggle.'

A higher profile and recognition in public is also being enjoyed by Dr Finlay's new partner, the upstart Dr David Neil – fresh out of Edinburgh University and confident he has the answers to what ails everyone in Tannochbrae – played by Jason Flemyng. For Jason, at just twenty-six and still very much making his way in the profession, appearing in the series has resulted in the kind of exposure that may well significantly influence the rest of his career.

'When you've been working in a wine bar one day and then a short while later wake up to find headlines in the *Sun*: "FRIDAYS

RUIN NOOKIE FOR FINLAY ROOKIE," you know things have really changed in your life,' the lanky young actor with his waves of reddish-blonde hair and intense dark eyes told me, flashing one of the engaging smiles that has made him such a favourite with female viewers. Indeed, there is something of the early Peter O'Toole about this young man with his driving ambition and self-deprecating sense of humour.

Dr Neil is the only major character in *Doctor Finlay* who was not present in the BBC original series. But his ability to regularly rub his partner up the wrong way and some-how still avoid the sort of disasters his impetu-osity could lead to, have enabled Jason to develop the part and become more than just a makeweight in the quartet of stars.

The *Sun*'s story in April 1993 claimed that 'heart-throb' Jason was being plagued by female fans, but that they were all housewives and youngsters because girls of his age were out at night clubs on Fridays, when *Doctor Finlay* was being screened. He wanted it moved to Sunday night, he said, so that his love life might improve. Jason was quoted as saying:

'*When I go out for a few beers, no-one*

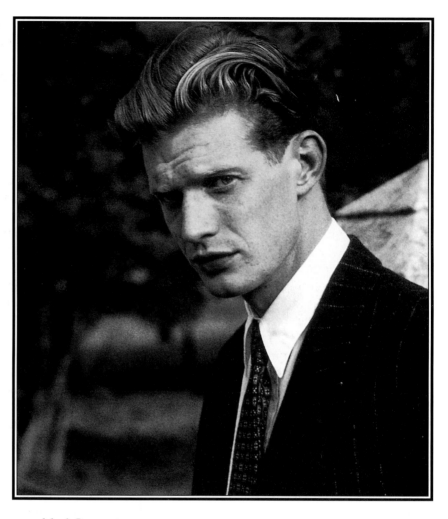

Jason Flemyng as Dr David Neil.

seems to notice me. But you should hear the comments I get shopping in the super-market on Saturday mornings. A lot of ladies shout I should be nicer to Dr Finlay. But they all seem to be married or schoolkids, which isn't much use to a young, free and single guy like me.'

Coping with the changes that playing Dr Neil have brought to Jason's life has undoubtedly been helped by his background: his father is the veteran television director, Gordon Flemyng

(*The Younger Generation, Burgess, Philby and Maclean*, etc) while his mother, Fiona, was a dancer on Scottish television in the programme *One O'Clock Gang*, where the couple met.

'My parents actually divorced when I was young, so my brother Gareth and I were basically brought up by my mother,' he says candidly. 'She was great. She worked days as a secretary and had a night job, too. She struggled, like a lot of people do in those circumstances, but she has given me lots of encouragement in my work. It was really nice for her to come back to Scotland when I started work on *Doctor Finlay*. She opened STV – and I think I'm going to close it!'

Although both his parents are Scottish, Jason was born and raised in England. And, unlike his co-stars, he never saw the original series. 'When I started work on *Doctor Finlay*, it was just a new drama series to me,' he explains. 'Probably forty or fifty percent of the population had never seen the original either. So when people were saying things like, "It won't be as good as the first one", I couldn't answer them because I hadn't even been born then. What I did say was that since anyone under thirty had probably never seen or heard it either, and it was going out on Friday night, a lot of them probably wouldn't be around to see it this time as well. So really it was only those who had watched the original who could now compare it with *Doctor Finlay*.

For such a young actor, Jason has packed a variety of work into his life. He got interested in acting when he was at primary school and then won a scholarship to Christ's Hospital in Sussex. This was followed by a boarding school at Horsham. 'The school had a brilliant theatre,' he recalls. 'I was really into the drama classes because I wanted to be a stunt man, but I just didn't have the bottle for it. Instead, I became a bit of a rebel and got myself thrown out for selling communion wine. We were nicking it and selling it to the other kids. But believe me, it was the kind of school where you could get chucked out for not doing your top button up.'

Not to be deterred from his ambition to act, he enrolled at a drama school in London and then managed to get an apprenticeship at the Royal Shakespeare Company. 'I spent fifteen months there, spear-carrying and understudying the big roles, but I never got a chance to do any of them. But I did watch the leads drinking until three or four o'clock in the morning and then still turn up, hung over, but on stage. I thought, "This is for me!" '

It was television that offered Jason his first break. He made an impressive début playing the traitor Anthony Blunt's assistant in Alan Bennett's *A Question of Attribution*, which was directed by John Schlesinger and won a BAFTA award. Jason's other appearances included *Lovejoy* and a 'very lucrative' stint in a TV commercial for a chain of petrol stations which he prefers not to name.

'Then I spent some time in Prague in the *Young Indy* based on George Lucas's *Indiana Jones* movies. I was Indy Jones' trench pirate who taught him the ropes. It was after that I auditioned for *Doctor Finlay*.'

Jason runs his hands through his thick head of red hair and grins at the memory. 'Peter Wolfes is a very brave man,' he said. 'A lot of producers and directors will look at you, and although you know they like you, because you haven't a proven record they're just not prepared to give you a chance. That is until you find someone like Peter who will take a chance.

'We actually met in London, and I'm sure that when he went back to STE and said that he'd found Dr Neil, he was a cockney from South London and he hadn't done much, they must have freaked out a bit! Anyhow, when I got the offer, I couldn't believe it. I was working in a wine bar in Battersea, near where I lived at the

(Above) *Dr Finlay gives the inexperienced Dr Neil some advice.*

(Left) *David Neil in a mischievous mood with friend Annie (Hilary McLean).*

clearly based on actual experience.

Jason obviously liked the challenge of coming to a part without a precedent for the character attached to it from the previous series, and I asked him about the flurry of press stories which accompanied his début, claiming he had based his accent on that of the well-

time. I just threw in my dish towel and stormed up to Scotland. I was really chuffed and I must admit I had a small celebration.'

Despite the fact he had been raised in England, Jason had grown up with the sound of his mother's strong accent. 'I was very conscious of the fact that I had to justify being English and doing a job which is a Scottish part, but all my life I've heard my mother's voice, and I have an ear for the accent,' he said, demonstrating with an instant and hilarious imitation of a 'wee wifey' bawling out one of her children,

Will romance blossom between Neil and Annie?

known Scottish MP, Sir David Steel.

'Yes, I did listen to a tape of David Steel because it was the kind of accent I thought of working towards,' he explained. 'But there was more to it than that. In television, the preparation time before filming is very short, and it was about five days before shooting that they told me they wanted me to try the role doing an Edinburgh accent. I did work quite hard for a couple of days, but then decided against it.

'When you are going to play a role like Dr Neil, which will last for twelve hour-long episodes, you know that the accent you use on the first day of shooting is the one you are going to have to live with. It is such a long time to commit to, and once you reach that period when you begin to get tired and you are really having to work on the lines, the last thing you need is to be strangled by an accent which you find difficult. So I talked to Peter Wolfes about it and he said, "Do one you are comfortable with." The result is an accent which has a slight David Steel influence, but is really just posh Glasgow.'

Getting into the role of Dr David Neil himself was rather easier. 'I think he is me with a Scottish accent sitting up straight,' Jason laughed. 'I'm not an actor who does a huge transformation, but I hope I'm a truthful one. Everything I do I try to find from within myself.

'Dr Neil is young and opinionated and, to begin with, Finlay feels he's there merely because of his father's money. He can behave a bit like a bull in a china shop, too. Actually, he's a lot posher and more Scottish than me, of course, because I like to dress casually and hang around the bars of London. You have to pay attention to the period, too. You can't walk around looking like a pimp from south London! For the last two years, I seem to have played a succession of Cockney wide-boys,' he added. 'Mum said she didn't bring me up to speak like that, so she was really pleased when I got the part of David Neil.'

Aside from the doctor's accent and appearance, he has also had to demonstrate a certain medical expertise on screen. 'I've had terrible trouble getting the medical terms right,' he confessed. 'I seem to get them wrong every time. Mind you, I believe the series is more about the characters than the fact they are doctors. *Doctor Finlay* is not like *Casualty*, where the drama comes from what they do; it comes from the situations in which they find themselves. I haven't quite been able to get over how positively barbaric some of the surgical equipment was. It was so bulky and fearsome-looking.'

The conversation at this point suddenly reminded Jason of an incident during the filming of the first series. 'In the second episode, David and I were carrying out an urgent procedure on a wee girl to remove fluid from her heart. Obviously, we couldn't go sticking needles into her, so we had to inject a substitute. And I have to tell you, it is difficult to look really concerned and anxious when you are staring down at a sickly-looking turnip!'

Jason acknowledges his debt to his three much more experienced co-stars. 'I'm not cocky confident,' he says, 'but because I stood behind a lot of talented people at the RSC and watched them, I felt able to cope. I just worked out for myself that the best way to be in this business when you don't know what you are doing, is to keep honest, keep your eyes open and watch what people are doing.

'Ian Bannen in particular made me nervous to begin with because I admire his work. But it's not a problem any more. The trouble was, I was trying too hard to make the scenes really work. I mean, if you try to compete with Ian and play games with him when he is working, he'll blow you out of the water. Ian carries you through scenes, literally. As long as you respond to what he does honestly, then it makes you look good as well.'

Despite his undoubted impact in the first two series of *Doctor Finlay*, Jason will not be appearing in any further episodes. He has already decided to leave the show. Why?

'I know some people will say I'm crazy, but I think it is the right thing for me to do. I didn't become an actor to get used to financial security, because it gets too comfortable and you start picking parts for the wrong reason. I don't want to sound conceited, but I also don't want to start repeating myself. In the second series of any type of drama, you inevitably have to repeat situations. In Arden House, we have classic scenes recurring, involving breakfast and Janet bringing in the tray and that sort of thing. I am very young and I just want to

keep on going, and I'm greedy for work and new experiences.'

He paused a moment and then added: 'I work best when I'm really scared. I try and get myself as wound up as I can. I remember that Patrick Lau, who is a brilliant director, taking time to work out what you need and give it to you, said on a couple of occasions that I get myself *too* wound up. He explained that I was not winding up Dr Neil for the scene, I was winding up Jason and that was getting in the way.'

An actual manifestation of this was Jason's habit of pinching his cheeks and flapping his hands just before shooting a scene. This mannerism was soon noticed by other members of the cast and crew and, unbeknownst to him, the actions were being mimicked behind his back by David Rintoul and Ian Bannen. A selection of out-takes of these little jokes were shown to Jason just before he left the series and afforded him enormous amusement.

'I had no idea that stuff was so obvious to everyone,' he said, grinning at the memory. 'But it does show you how close David, Ian, Annette and I became. I'm obviously going to miss working with them all, but I'm always interested in what is over the horizon. Financially, it has been very nice, but I'm not used to money and it is not a need for me because I'm not married and don't have a family. At the end of the day, I've acted since I was ten and I've never earned any money from it, so I decided before I got used to it, perversely, that I'd get out. And now, of course, I might have the time to meet that gorgeous girl I've been waiting for!'

The series may not have brought love into Jason Flemyng's life, but it certainly has into the screen characters of his other two co-stars. And the romance which as blossomed between Janet, the housekeeper, and Tannochbrae's chemist, Angus Livingstone –

Chapter Seven

ROMANCE COMES TO
TANNOCHBRAE

HERE HAS BEEN ROMANCE IN THE AIR in Tannochbrae all through the new series of *Doctor Finlay*. It began to exert its seductive powers in the first six episodes: initially, with Finlay's attraction to a married woman after his fiancée had jilted him for a GI, and then, more surprisingly, involving Janet MacPherson, the indispensable housekeeper of Arden House. In the second series, the relationship between Janet and the local chemist, Angus, has become an altogether much stronger element, with the prospect of marriage in sight.

The romance was particularly evident in the streets of Auchtermuchty, during the summer of 1993, where some of the crucial scenes were being filmed of the meetings between the two lovers and the heart-searching of Dr Cameron, a silent and perhaps even regretful witness to the developing relationship. They were all played with consummate skill by three highly professional actors, each bringing a lifetime of experience to their roles.

The relationship between the housekeeper and the local shopkeeper has been developed with particular sensitivity by Annette Crosbie and Gordon Reid, and so convincing were they on camera that coming across the couple having dinner together at the end of one day's shooting made me feel, for just an instant, like an intruder upon a private matter. The presence of Ian Bannen in the same hotel likewise seemed to add frisson to the notion of a 'love triangle' behind the series.

The introduction of an affair into Janet's life has made special demands on Annette Crosbie's portrayal of the housekeeper, the 'little body' forever remembered from the original series as a prim and proper housekeeper, more adept at serving tea and sympathy than indulging in lovers' smalltalk. The decision to widen the housekeeper's life beyond her kitchen sink was taken right at the outset.

'Television, like life, must move on,' said Peter Wolfes. 'The Twenties, the era of the original series were very proper times; things became much freer in the post-war Britain of the Forties. And because we are always seeing *young* love on the screen, I thought it would be brave to show two people in their fifties fall in love. We shouldn't forget that people *did* fall in love and have sex in those days, too.'

Annette Crosbie, Peter's first and only choice as Janet, is a private person, whose seeming brusqueness on first meeting actually masks a deeply concerned attitude towards life and a capability for the warmest of friendships with fellow actors and film crew members. At the moment, she is one of the most high-profile actresses on television as the oppressed Margaret Meldrew, wife of the awful moaner Victor (Richard Wilson) in the award-winning BBC comedy *One Foot In The Grave*, and as

ON CALL WITH DOCTOR FINLAY

Annette Crosbie as housekeeper Janet MacPherson.

her very caring nature.

'I think it is understandable that people want to hark back to a better time,' she said on one of those occasions, her firmly-modulated voice still betraying her Scottish origins, although she has lived in London for many years, 'because the world we are all trying to cope with at the moment is just so awful. What we want are times of moral certitude. I just don't understand how people can go stealing cars, raping, breaking into old people's homes or mugging a woman of eighty for a few pounds. No wonder the nostalgia of shows like *Doctor Finlay* is so addictive. We are all hankering back to a time when life was nicer and sweeter, kinder and gentler.'

Janet in *Doctor Finlay*. But despite these and all her other achievements, Annette has an aversion to giving interviews and prefers to be judged by the public on her performances.

'I don't like answering questions, because I'm no good at it,' she told me when we were first introduced during a lunch break in Auchtermuchty. 'I'm not Glenda Jackson. I'm not articulate and coherent. I wish to God I were. However, several subsequent impromptu conversations with her in the town, over a meal and sharing a taxi after a night out with the cast and crew, enabled me to see and appreciate both her dedication to her work and

Annette's contribution to the series has gone much further than helping to bring a pleasant bygone era to life, for she has also recreated a television icon. And although it might be said that her costume, of a flower pattern pinny worn over a calf-length skirt, can evoke memories of her predecessor, the face is more resolute, the eyes more knowing and the smile is certainly more dazzling.

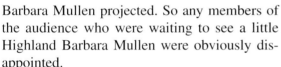

The unspoken attachment between Janet and Dr Cameron runs deeper than either will admit.

'Of course, I was chary about taking over the part,' she said, admitting that she had watched some of the original episodes of *Dr Finlay's Casebook.* 'But my Janet was never going to be the same as the one Barbara Mullen projected. So any members of the audience who were waiting to see a little Highland Barbara Mullen were obviously disappointed.

'This Janet is, I suppose, more me. In the old series, Janet didn't have an interest outside the practice. She used to be the wee wifey who had to do things through a kind of devious manipulation. In those days, women didn't have that kind of authority or say in anything.

'I cannot be as fey as I gather Barabara was; I am a woman of a new time. My Janet has had to keep the practice running while a World War was being fought. She would have known people who were killed and suffered the grief. She would have needed a mind of her own to survive.

'But now she has come through the hard times and she is more sure of herself. She is strong and much more independent. She's not a raging feminist or anything like that, but she is more of her own woman. She wants a little comfort in her life, too, and that's where Alex the chemist comes in.'

Once the subject of *Doctor Finlay* and today's social issues have been discussed, it is harder to extract information from Annette about her own life. Fortunately, though, the highlights are well documented. She was born in 1934 in Gorebridge, but grew up in Edinburgh, first in Pilton and then Gilmerton. Her father was an insurance agent and both parents apparently nursed ambitions for her to be a piano tutor.

'My folks were not church-going,' she says. 'But you know, if you are in Scotland, it's in the genes. You are a Calvinist. It's just the air you breathe; it's the way you are programmed. I don't think you can budge that; theoretically you can try, but emotionally there you are: you are guilty for the rest of your life.'

As a pupil at Boroughmuir High School, she did display an appetite for the piano and competed in a number of music contests. However, all she really wanted to do was act. 'The school didn't know what to make of me, but I don't think I was a particularly rebellious teenager. Rather like Janet in this series, I had to find my fun in the aftermath of war, and a solitary coffee shop in Shandwick Place offered just about all the fun that could be had in Edinburgh at that time.'

Dr Finlay's Casebook:

BARBARA MULLEN:
'FIRST LADY OF TANNOCHBRAE'

ALTHOUGH, IN HER ROLE AS JANET, Barbara Mullen always appeared to be the archetypal Scots 'wee wifey', she was actually born on the Arran Islands off the coast of Galway on 9 June 1914 and was raised in Boston, Massachusetts. This I remember, was not the only surprise that confronted me when I met Barbara at her home in Stamford Brook, London, in the summer of 1975. For she greeted me at the door with a cigarette in her hand and, once indoors, confessed that among her favourite roles had been playing a fairy queen and a sex maniac. It was on the tip of my tongue to ask what Janet would have thought of such behaviour, but I quickly learned that Barbara was actually a very different woman to her television persona.

'I may have unconsciously grown a bit like Janet during the years we were making the series,' she said to me, 'but acting is my life, and I am always an actress playing a role. If I wasn't, then I would be scanning the domestic situations looking for a housekeeping job.' The mischievous grin that crossed her deceptively mild face, with its halo of white hair, made it clear to me that here was a woman with a strong sense of humour and a very down-to-earth attitude towards life. An attitude that she had developed during a childhood that was tough, by any standards.

'When you're living it you don't notice it,' she reminisced. 'I was only a baby when my parents left Ireland and moved to South Boston. There we lived through the horrors of the Depression in a mixed race community of Irish, Jewish, Polish and Chinese. After a while, my father, Pat, went back to Ireland and left my mother with ten children to feed.

'People say now that we're going through a recession,' she continued, 'but they don't know what it means. My mother used to hold dances in the house to save the family of a child, who had died from malnutrition, from the ultimate degradation of a pauper's grave. People would come to watch and pay what they could at the door. It was called "Dancing for a Coffin".'

Barbara was educated at an experimental school in Boston run by Catholic nuns, all of whom had studied at the Sorbonne. Her first language was Irish, and her second Chinese. She learned English, with the lilting Scots accent that she would use so effectively in *Dr Finlay's Casebook*, from the parish priest. In 1934, she achieved her ambition and arrived in Ireland to find her father starring in Robert Flaherty's classic documentary film, *Man of Aran*. It was all the inspiration she needed to set off for London, where she underwent two years formal training at drama school before making her début in 1939. This extra polishing of a natural talent, combined with the hard-won experience of life, proved an immediate help to Barbara, who became a star almost literally overnight in the 1940 stage production of *Jeannie*.

Television became a growing feature in her career when she appeared in adaptations of *Juno and the Paycock* and in *The Danny Thomas Show*. Those who now hailed her as a new star of TV, were unaware that she had actually first appeared in the medium as early as 1938, dancing in an Irish programme transmitted live from Alexandra Palace. She therefore had no hesitation in accepting the role of Janet when the series was mooted in 1962.

'I had been appearing on TV since before the war, so a new series, even a Scottish one, was just a new challenge,' she told me. 'I think they chose me because the producer genuinely believed I was Scottish. Obviously, I was glad of the work, though I didn't think it would last very long.'

Over a decade later she was able to revise that verdict and consider the intervening years.

'Although Janet only had two lines in one of the intended six episodes, I wanted to do it because it was about something from my own experience,' she said. 'The subject was diphtheria and I could remember a time when diphtheria had come up our street like a plague, and no one was saved from it. It was so real in memory and I couldn't forget it.

'It was a painful time and I saw a lot of

death. But there was a lot of joy, too. The people who were alive were glad to be alive – it was a bonus. It was an even greater bonus to be able to work for a living. Many of the fathers suffered terribly from the Depression disease, which is being unable to support your family. We used to pray for snow so the men would get a day's work shovelling it. Things like that keep your feet on the ground. It reminds us we are all mortal.'

While neither Bill Simpson or Andrew Cruikshank had any reason to believe they would become famous as the result of the new series, Barbara, with two lines, had even less reason to think her humble role would make her a household name. Yet thanks to a mixture of public demand and her own brilliant characterization of Janet the housekeeper, forever keeping a cool and sensible mind amidst imminent medical disaster, and at the same time acting as the calming influence between the impetuous Finlay and crusty Dr Finlay, she became as central to the success story as her two co-stars. Her antidote to the direst of situations also became a catch phrase throughout the nation: 'A cup of tea, Dr Finlay?'; and within a year the press were referring to her affectionately as, 'The white haired treasure of Arden House, the impeccable ruler of the Cameron-Finlay roost.'

Barbara enjoyed the trips to Callander for location shooting, and was always a welcome visitor to the Crags Hotel. Her reputation as something of a joker still survives to this day in a story which has been retold endlessly. Despite the fact that she had listed her hobbies in one biography as 'fishing, writing, darts and arguing', no one in the bar was aware of the fact, when she innocently asked some of the locals one night if they fancied a game for a round of drinks. Looking as if she might be an easy touch, the challenge was taken up at once. Barbara asked Bill Simpson to partner her. 'It was just a bit of fun,' one resident was to recall later, 'but it was the locals who were surprised. Barbara and Bill didn't have to buy a drink all night!'

As the tears passed, Barbara also subtly changed Janet's character in a way that passed almost unnoticed. 'It was quite deliberate,' she told me. 'Janet gained more strength of character and a little more inner maturity. It was a gentle change to keep pace with the years. If people didn't see it happening I must have got it about right,'

Looking back, five years after she removed the trappings of the little housekeeper for the last time, she reflected. 'A bit of oneself rubs off on to every part and a bit of the part rubs off on to you. But you're still mainly yourself. The real me is only small in size. I'm a very commonsensical character. My family call me the Rock.'

Away from the cameras, Barbara enjoyed a happy marriage to film producer, John Taylor, and the couple raised two daughters, Bridget and Susannah. All three were enthusiasts of *Dr Finlay's Casebook*, but never ceased to pull her leg whenever she inadvertently came out with an expression at home that they had heard her use in the series. Like her co-stars, Bill and Andrew, she continued in the BBC radio version of *Dr Finlay's Casebook* until it, too, finished in the autumn of 1978.

A few short months later, on 9 March 1979, Barbara sadly became the first of the trio to die, after having been admitted a few days earlier to Hammersmith Hospital. Most of the obituaries in the following day's newspapers were a mirror of the *Daily Telegraph*'s, 'Dr Finlay's Housekeeper Dies', or the *Glasgow Herald*'s poignant description of her as, 'The First Lady of Tannochbrae'.

It was an accolade well deserved by an actress who had overcome the odds of a deprived childhood and a hard life, to create one of the gentlest, most respected and enduring female characters on television.

Annette Crosbie, Edith McArthur (as Izabel Gant) and Anne Kristen (as Rachel Gant) on set.

When Annette announced to her parents that she wanted to be an actress, their reaction was one of total horror. 'I think my Dad saw it a bit like going into prostitution. But my piano teacher encouraged me and found someone to apply for a grant, and I managed to save on it.'

Annette has vivid memories of growing up during the war years in Edinburgh, memories on which she has been able to draw for *Doctor Finlay*. Her actual first step into acting took place when she was seventeen and she joined the Bristol Old Vic, where one of her contemporaries was Peter O'Toole. Two years later, she gained entry to the Old Vic in London and understudied Dame Wendy Hiller. In 1956 she had her big break when she co-starred with Alistair Sim in *Mr Bolfry* in the West End.

She has subsequently earned a reputation as one of Britain's finest character actresses and among her achievements have been three BAFTA awards, playing Catherine of Aragon in *The Six Wives of Henry VIII* (BBC, 1971), Queen Victoria in *Edward VII* (ITV, 1976), and most recently, of course, Janet MacPherson in *Doctor Finlay*. But she has never enjoyed the celebrity and publicity that such recognition brings.

'It's just ludicrous to single out one actor for praise when success has been a team effort,' Annette said on one occasion, after having shared her mid-day meal with several members of the film crew. The jokes and banter between them clearly showed that she wanted to be treated no differently to anyone else working on *Doctor Finlay*, and more than once emphasized to me the importance of everyone's contribution to the series. Then she added: 'Personal publicity just serves to perpetuate the myth that show business is really important, which it isn't.'

Annette will not, though, let the team down by refusing to co-operate on publicity. 'It's just something I have to try to put up with, I suppose. The people who just stare at me are the ones I find difficult to handle. I smile back, but usually they don't smile back, they go on staring.'

Annette insists that she always has to conquer stage-fright whenever she is performing and has been quoted as saying: 'I almost always look inwards at myself and there I find fear. I am a jelly of inadequacy.' A remark she made about her character Margaret Meldrew is perhaps even more illuminating: 'The woman is a saint. I don't know why she's not on tranquillizers. I can't say I'm like her in the least. I'm more like Victor: frustrated by life's inadequacies. I am very intolerant and impatient.'

Although Annette was married for twenty-two years, she is now divorced but remains close to her ex-husband, Michael, and has two children: Owen, a recording engineer, and Selina, who is hoping to follow in her mother's footsteps as an actress. Annette lives in a modest house in Wimbledon and has a great affection for animals, in particular the latest addition: a retired greyhound, photographs of which she carries everywhere.

She worries about both the human and animal members of her family, and her peace of mind was disturbed recently by the murder of model Rachel Nickell, at a spot on Wimbledon Common which her son and daughter pass and where she regularly walks her two dogs. 'London isn't a place to live in anymore, ' she says. 'It's just a huge metropolis that attracts a lot of tourism.'

In the light of this remark, I was not surprised at her answer when I asked her over lunch one day the reason for her accepting the role of Janet. 'I've wanted to come back to Scotland for ages,' she said. 'I have spent most of my time in London because that's where most of the work is. But Scotland is my home and it's lovely being able to spend some time here during the filming.'

When I followed this up by asking what had appealed to her about the role, she fixed me with one of her direct and uncompromising stares and said, 'I'm fifty-eight years old and I've been in the business for thirty-six years. I don't think in those terms anymore. I need the work and I need the money. It's as basic as that. I'm an actress who responds to the lines of the script. That's how I work.'

She has found the relationship of Janet and Angus interesting to play, and is naturally curious to see how its development will be received by the viewers. The outcome has been left intriguingly open at the end of the second series for the third, which has already been commissioned by STV.

'Janet's relationship with the pharmacist is what you might call an "arrangement",' she is quoted in STE's publicity brochure. 'We're talking '46 village romance here, and neither of them is a chicken. But it does have an influence on surgery life.'

Just what kind of an influence I found out from, first, Gordon Reid, and then Dr Cameron himself...

Annette Crosbie with Margo Gunn, Jason Flemyng, David Rintoul and Gordon Reid on location in Auchtermuchty.

Gordon Reid, a small, immaculate man with an impish sense of humour, has two very good qualifications for playing Angus Livingstone, Tannochbrae's chemist and the man in Janet's life. His father was a Scottish doctor who operated a surgery next door to a pharmacy, and Gordon's television début was actually in the original *Dr Finlay's Casebook*.

The rapport which Gordon has struck up with Annette in the series has evolved from their own friendship off camera and the development of both their characters on screen. Gordon has, in fact, been with the series from the start and brings a wealth of practical experience, from his own early years, to the life of a small-town chemist in the aftermath of war. We talked both in the streets of Auchtermuchty and inside the pharmacy, which was stacked high with packets of long-forgotten medical preparations form Robert Opie's collection, including 'Meggason' ('Stops Palpitations And Flatulence'), 'Genasprin' ('For Summer Headaches') and 'Virolax' ('The Nutrient Laxative').

'This place is a bit like home,' Gordon told me, smoothing down his chemist's white overall. 'Certainly, it brings back memories of my childhood.

My father was a doctor and he had two surgeries. One was next door to our house in Wishaw, Lanarkshire, which was where he saw his better-off patients. The other was in Craigneuk, right next door to a chemist. That was for the poor, the unemployed, the halt and the lame who couldn't afford to go to Wishaw, and so had to travel there.

'The pharmacy was actually run by two spinster ladies and they also took all the bookings for my father's surgery. I went to Craigneuk with him quite a lot. I remember that in Wishaw, too, there were people who

*Gordon Reid as Angus
Livingstone, the local chemist.*

could not afford to go to the doctor. So if they had something serious, they would go to the chemist and ask what he could do for the complaint. Chemists could diagnose a lot of things and they were actually far more important in the community than they often given credit for.'

Like co-star David Rintoul, Gordon never considered following his father's profession, or that of a chemist. Acting was his passion, and he studied at the Glasgow Drama School until 1962. After that, he did three years in rep at Stoke-on-Trent before heading for the big metropolis of London where he had heard there were openings in the fast developing medium of television.

'I got my very first big break with the BBC when they cast me in an episode of *Dr Finlay's Casebook* in 1965,' Gordon said. 'I played this young lad named Archie who was dying of TB. The series was still being made in London then, and we rehearsed in an old drill hall in the Brompton Road. When I arrived, they gave me a bed and told me to lie down. The next thing I knew, the other actors were coming back from lunch and I had obviously fallen asleep.'

Gordon laughs at the memory of trying to collect his wits, as the director, Moira Armstrong – who would later become famous for her production of *Testament of Youth* (1979), the story of Vera Brittain written by another *Dr Finlay's Casebook* scriptwriter, Elaine Morgan – approached him with the star, Andrew Cruikshank.

'Moira came over to where I was laying in bed. "Oh, Andrew," she said, "have you met Gordon Reid?" Before I could do anything, he just said, "How do you do?", and put his stethoscope on my chest and went straight into the scene. That was my first meeting with the great man and also my introduction to acting for television,' he said.

Gordon has subsequently appeared in a number of productions directed by Moira Armstrong, but had not worked with Scottish Television until 1992 when he was cast in an episode of *Taggart*. He says that getting the role of Angus Livingstone was just a case of being in Glasgow when the series was being set up. 'I got the part because I'm not too tall,' he grinned. 'I'm the right age, fifty-three, and I'm Scots. They are probably running out of Scots actors of my generation and this is my turn. I *am* Angus!'

Gordon has, in fact, already become very much identified with the role, and although he won't go into details, says a similar relationship has also developed in his personal life. His lady friend has, he claims, helped him in building up a believable relationship between Janet and Angus.

'You can imagine the two of them falling in love, can't you?' he said; but before I could reply he was called away to film a scene in the shop with Annette. When he came back, I turned the conversation to the development of Angus as a character.

'Well, the storyline for him is basically very sketchy in terms of background,' he says. 'In fact, it was quite clear in Episode One that Angus did not know Dr Finlay at all. So, on the assumption that Finlay had gone off to war in 1940–1 and returned, meeting the chemist for the first time, Angus was obviously not from Tannochbrae. So I decided to make up his background myself.

'It is a difficult and dangerous situation to be put into the position of making love to a character like Janet. There was such a strong impression of her in many people's minds from the original BBC series. Even though ours was a completely new programme and she was a spinster, it was still very important to handle the affair with delicacy. I remember one of the very first things Annette said to me

Janet and Angus, with whom she has an 'understanding'.

knowledge of the life of such a person could be exploited and cites an example where it proved invaluable.

'In one episode, my attractive niece, Rhona (played by Jackie Morrison) was sitting on the counter and her legs naturally distracted a male customer. I said that under no circumstances would a chemist in those days, in that kind of society have allowed such a thing to happen.'

For the time being, however, Gordon has been happy to play out the relationship of the couple, through their engagement, to the climax in the last episode of the second series which is their wedding day.

'The love interest of Angus and Janet is soap,' he says philosophically. 'But while it is just an element of Janet, it is almost the total element of me. That's why I'd like them to involve me more in the community. Still who knows what might be in store in the third series? I was having a joke with Annette the other day and suggested that the new series might be a continuation of the wedding. The minister would say, "Does anyone know of any lawful impediment?", and before I could get out what I was going to say, Annette said: "Yes, a wee wifey will jump up and shout, That's my husband!" ' We both laugh at the suggestion and then Gordon is serious for a final thought. 'The last thing we want to see is

when we were waiting for the first shoot: "Has Angus been married before?" And I said, "Yes, I'm a widower."

'I decided that Angus had come from another town somewhere to the east of Tannochbrae. After the death of his wife, he was one of those people who just had to get out and move on. That's how he came to the town and took over the pharmacy. As to the affair, if you suddenly start talking about a confirmed bachelor getting lusty for a spinster, I wouldn't believe it and I don't think the audience would either. Ours is essentially middle-aged love and it *does* happen.'

Gordon would naturally like to see his role enlarged in the series, because he believes that the chemist has a role in places like Tannochbrae that was important socially, economically and politically. He also feels his

ROMANCE COMES TO TANNOCHBRAE

Ian Bannen as Dr Alexander Cameron.

Janet and Angus between the sheets!'

The idea of Janet in bed with a man is certainly not one that the original Dr Cameron would have contemplated; and the thought is also somewhat disconcerting to his reincarnation, although the reservations of the latter could well be described as more personal.

It seemed very appropriate to me that the last of the stars of *Doctor Finlay* whom I talked to should be Ian Bannen, the man playing the wise and unflappable Dr Cameron and one of the major figures in the ranks of our leading actors. All the more so, because it brought my research into the legend of Dr Finlay full circle. For not only had Ian been offered the role of the young GP in the original BBC series, but he also returned to his home town of Coatbridge a few miles outside Glasgow to film the climactic scenes of Janet's wedding day, at which he was to give the bride away.

Watching Ian at work on location, it was clear to see he was comfortable in the role of Cameron, but it was impossible not to wonder just how he might have handled the younger role of Finlay, thirty years ago. My first sight of him was in a scene where Cameron discovers an advertisement put by Janet in the newsagent's window, seeking a replacement. Peering through the window at the card, the doctor's face expressed an inner emotion that was clearly deeper than he had expected...

HOUSEKEEPER WANTED
Full-time appointment
Apply in writing only to:
Arden House,
Tannochbrae.

When we met to talk later, Ian was relaxing in a track suit and trainers. There is a brooding presence about him, and although now in his sixties with a distinguished career that spans over forty years, his eyes are never still and his voice has a penetrating rumble that demands attention. His craggy features can also be a mask at one moment – his sharp nose almost an accusation and his mouth set in a grim line – and then dissolve into an affable and amused smile. It is all part of the persona that has made him such a formidable and widely-acclaimed actor. He seated himself comfortably and then began to talk about his childhood, his career and his long association with *Dr Finlay*.

'I grew up in this part of Scotland, so it has been like coming home to work here,' he said. 'My family actually owned some land in Coatbridge which is named Bannen's Land. My grandfather was in the scrap metal business and, like a lot of dealers, he made a fortune. He bought up quite a large portion of Coatbridge and handed it down to my father. The last will we can find shows that the land was willed to *all* his children, including my father. But there doesn't seem to be one after that which isolates exactly what the beneficiaries should receive. So now we are busy trying to get the lawyers to sort things out, as there are people who want to buy some of the land to build houses on.'

A laugh splits the silence as Ian thinks of the implications of being a Scottish laird. He turns to his own childhood. 'It was a lot harder to get around in Scotland fifty years ago. My father was a lawyer and his favourite hobby was walking, so he never learned to drive a car. I think he walked over most of Scotland before he got married, late in life. So we were reliant on the SMT [Scottish Motor Transport] buses, which were slow and always breaking down. We usually came through the Auchtermuchty district when we were going on holiday to St Andrews, which we did frequently.

When he was twelve, Ian was sent away to boarding school on England ('it was terrible, I nearly starved to death') and then appropriately in 1946, the year in which *Doctor Finlay* is set, a chance meeting set him on the career which has since made him a household name.

'It was just after the war and I had finished college,' he said, another smile beginning to spread over his craggy features at the memory. 'I went on holiday to Dublin and there I fell in with a chap who said he knew a producer's wife who would be able to introduce us to some young actresses. Well, we ended up having dinner at her house and she asked me if I'd ever done any acting. I thought there was nothing to lose, so I auditioned at the Gate Theatre and the next thing, there I was, a Scot, making my acting début in Dublin.'

Before Ian could take his career any further, however, he was called up to do his National Service in the army. 'They put me in public relations. I happened to be in Egypt when the official photographer gave up and as I had a camera, they gave me the job and let me get on with it. I've never had such a good time! When I left the army I was a bit torn between the two professions.'

In fact, he opted for the stage and almost at once his career took off. He joined the Royal Shakespeare Company in 1951 and struck up an immediate friendship with Richard Burton. The two young actors shared digs, and Ian remembers that Burton gave him some of the best advice he ever had. 'I was a bit worried that I'd never had any proper training to be an actor. Then Richard asked me one day if I'd gone to drama school. When I said I hadn't, he replied: "Good – you don't want to, either. You have a good regional accent, don't lose it." '

In 1956, Ian broke into films when he made the first of four pictures for the Boulting Brothers. He demonstrated his growing range in his subsequent movies which included a version of the classic *A Tale of Two Cities* (1958), *The Hill*, a violent drama about a military detention camp (1965), *The Flight of the Phoenix*, the gruelling tale of disaster and survival in the desert, for which he was nominated for an Oscar (1965), and Sidney Lumet's *The Offence* (1972) in which he played a suspected child molester pursued by Sean Connery as the policeman obsessively convinced of his guilt.

'That film was a bit ahead of its time,' Ian ruminated, 'but it's all too relevant now. Anyhow, many offers followed, not all of which I took up – a bit unwisely in retrospect. At the time, I thought Mike Caine was doing that, taking the money and running, but it didn't do him any harm at all. You see I had met this old producer who advised me: "Be careful what you do and what you take." He was totally wrong. I turned down so many top films that I got into the habit of it. I almost retired, living in extraordinary parts of Spain on the beach as though the offers would go on for ever. They dried up after a bit and I got exceedingly nervous and thought I had better start hustling.'

Among the parts which Ian rejected was that of Dr Finlay for the BBC. He chuckles when the subject is brought up and clearly remembers the time very well. 'In 1962, the BBC offered me the role and sent around six scripts for me to read,' he told me. 'A bit later, they asked me if I had read them. I said, "Yes, but they don't seem as much like Cronin as you said they were going to be. Not the Cronin I had read, anyway." I was disappointed, but I still went to see them to discuss the role.'

Ian says he had already read Cronin's novel, *The Citadel*, but was not told the series was being based on the author's autobiography and *The Adventures of a Black Bag*. He then paused and digressed for a moment, as he has a habit of doing when recounting his colourful life. 'An uncle of mine who was a radiologist was actually at college with AJ Cronin,' he revealed. 'I asked him once if there were any signs that he was going to be a great writer. Uncle Joe said: "I can't remember anything especially, except that once during a lecture we were asked to get up and read what we had written. And that particular day, Cronin got up and he quite spellbound us with what he had written." He was obviously a lovely essayist, even then.'

I drew Ian back to the subject of *Dr Finlay's Casebook*.

'After we had chatted for a bit, I said to the BBC people, "Look, what's the bottom line? What's the work schedule?" And they said, "You'll be working on Monday, Tuesday, Wednesday, Thursday and then recording on Friday. But you'll have Saturdays and Sundays off and start again on Monday." So I said, "When do I get time to learn the lines?" I know some people have photographic memories when it comes to learning a script, but I have always had to learn it line by line. So I decided it was all too much of a sweat and said no.'

Despite this refusal, Ian had quite clearly given some thought to how he might play the character, as he also revealed during our conversation. 'My first thought was of playing Dr Finlay much more aggressively,' he said, 'Bill Simpson played him more quietly and gently than I would have done. But I think now that I would have fared very badly against Andrew Cruikshank, unless the script had given us rows all the time.'

The mention of his predecessor's name

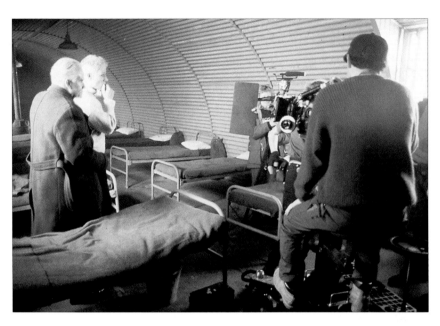

Ian Bannen during filming of a scene in a German POW camp.

prompted me to ask Ian if it was true that he had known Andrew Cruikshank as well. 'Oh, yes, he was a lovely man and very amusing,' Ian went on. 'He would say things to me like (and at this, the actor slipped into a perfect imitation of Cruikshank's thick Scots accent): "Eh, I've written a new play about the Duke of Hamilton and I'll send it to you. I'm sure we'll get it on in the West End. See what you think." I'd always read his plays, but he never managed to get them on the boards. I was very sorry about that.'

But Ian *was* to be associated with *Dr Finlay's Casebook*, albeit briefly. 'Although I'd turned them down, the BBC still offered me a part in one of the episodes, the following year.' he said. 'I played a miner, a nice big part. It was directed by Julia Smith who, of course, went on to become a top BBC executive with *EastEnders*. She was actually the daughter of a music teacher called Cuthbert

Smith who once tried to teach me. But so far, I haven't been asked to do West End musical!'

The episode in which Ian appeared as guest star, playing miner Rab Cunningham, was called 'Alice, Where Art Thou?' written by Alistair Bell. It was transmitted on 11 October 1963. 'I remember when I worked with Andrew that just before lunchtime, he would invite me to have a drink and a chat with him,' Ian continued, 'and as soon as he had drank one, he would say, "I'm off now, I'm just going to get my head down for a while." The part of Dr Cameron was tailor-made for him. In fact, I wouldn't have dreamt of playing Dr Finlay if I had known he was going to be in it and be so good.'

With hindsight, it seems probable that Ian's movie career might well not have taken off if he had committed himself to the series in the Sixties. 'So I really haven't got any regrets about turning it down, because I wouldn't have been able to do all those marvellous films. After the Oscar nomination, Hollywood took me into its arms and suddenly I was at parties with Judy Garland, thinking I had gone to the moon. I completely forgot about Finlay and Tannochbrae.'

Dr Finlay's Casebook is not, however, the only major TV-series role Ian rejected. He was offered the part of Steve McGarrett in the series *Hawaii Five-O* which made Jack Lord into an international celebrity.

'If a script is good I find it hard to say no,' he said. 'But when I read *Hawaii Five-O*,

I thought, "What nonsense!" I also thought it seemed far too American for me. Little did I know it was going to run for fifteen years or that it would all be filmed in Hawaii!'

How, then, did he react when the clock turned full circle and he was offered a part in the new *Doctor Finlay*?

'I have to admit, my first reaction was, "Oh, no, not again, I don't think so," ' he said. 'I think possibly I was also aware of how well Andrew had played the role. But I read the first three scripts and thought they were well-written and so I decided to have a crack at it. Perhaps I thought Andrew's shadow would be over me; certainly whenever I hear the name "Dr Cameron" I get this vivid image of the old chap. Anyway, I thought, "Bugger Andrew – I'm doing it." '

The reservations that Ian felt about being compared to Andrew Cruikshank were also felt at STE, and initially there were plans that unless he, or an actor of equal stature, could be found, then Dr Cameron might well have been retired completely from the series after only an episode or two. In fact, Ian Bannen has created his own unique characterization of the crotchety GP and become an essential ingredient in the success story of *Doctor Finlay*.

But two years on, does he have any cause for regrets at reversing his initial decision not to join the series?

'None at all,' he smiled. 'I suppose I was a bit wary about committing myself to a long-term television drama because there is always the chance it will clash with film offers. But the offer of such good television work is quite comforting and pleasing at my stage of life.

'I can't help unconsciously seeing

The two partners of Arden House.

ANDREW CRUIKSHANK AND THE 'CULT OF DR CAMERON'

T HE PUBLIC'S MEMORY of Andrew Cruikshank, as the wise but frequently irascible and cantankerous older partner, is as equally strong as that of Bill Simpson. Indeed, when he died less than two years later, after a lifetime in the theatre, in films and on television, it was for the role of Dr Cameron that he would be best remembered, said his obituaries.

'The BBC's legendary Casebook *might have been Dr Finlay's,'* declared the *Daily Mail, 'but its enduring star and symbol was Andrew Cruikshank, whose death from heart failure at the age of eighty leaves television, the stage, and life in general poorer. Along with Jack Warner's* Dixon of Dock Green, *crusty-yet-kindly Dr Cameron not only entertained millions, but stood for values which cheered and reassured them.'*

It was a role that he himself had enjoyed and remembered with affection throughout his life, as I recall him telling me when we met back in the Eighties at the modest flat he and his wife had shared for much of their lives, just behind Westminster Cathedral in London. He was as unforgettable a figure in life as he was when acting. Critic Frank Marcus once referred to him as being 'like a cross between Cecil King and a polar bear', and the remarkable set of mannerisms he perfected – chuckles, huffs, puffs, mumbles and grumbles – were as much a part of his everyday conversation as when he was delivering a piece of dialogue.

'I loved those years working on *Dr Finlay*,' he told me, sunk into a deep sofa, his head propped on a meaty fist. 'For me it was a delicious stint. I knew the pain of Scotland in the Twenties and I knew of medicine in the pre-Fleming days. It was very satisfying for an actor like myself to get back to the country of his roots.'

Andrew John Maxton Cruikshank was born on Christmas Day, 1908, in Aberdeen, the son of a sergeant in the Gordon Highlanders who later took over a hotel in Keith in Strathbogie. Despite plans

for a career in civil engineering at the age of twenty, he decided to leave Aberdeen and the Depression for the even more uncertain profession of show business. He joined a Shakespearean company which toured the provinces and ended up in London where a highlight was a walk-on part as a spear carrier in the memorable 1930 production of Othello, starring Paul Robeson.

It was in 1937 that Andrew appeared in his first television play, a production of Macbeth, broadcast from Alexandra Palace. The next year, he made his film début in *Auld Lang Syne*, and subsequently co-starred in the classic version of *The Cruel Sea* (with his great friend Jack Hawkins) and later still in the spectacular *El Cid*, with Charlton Heston.

In 1933 he had entered into what proved to be a tragically short marriage (his wife died within six months), but in 1939 he met and married the Welsh actress Curigwen Lewis, while both were appearing at the Old Vic. His career was interrupted by the war and, strangely for a Scot, he chose to serve in the Royal Welsh Fusiliers, ending up as a major. He was given an MBE in 1945.

It was in 1962 that *Dr Finlay* entered his life and the mantle for which he is best remembered settled on his shoulders. Curiously, for a man seen as an archetypal Scot, it was to be the first native role he had played since appearing at His Majesty's Theatre in Aberdeen as a child, and one of the very few he undertook during his long career.

'I was filming in Vienna at the time and the BBC sent me the first three *Dr Finlay* scripts,' he recalled. 'I said, I'd love to do it. We thought it was just a trial run of three, but then we all sort of settled into it. I've always liked playing doctors and judges: professional chaps always walk a moral tightrope between good and evil and it makes for a much more interesting part.'

Civilized inquiry had always been a central part of his life, Andrew explained, probably because he had never been an instinctive actor. He always had to wrestle with his parts, thinking them out. And also, as a deeply ingrained Scot with an appetite for service and knowledge, he felt this made him an ideal choice for Dr Cameron. 'It was like that when I grew up, and it just happened to suit my temperament,' he said. 'I make no claims for it, but it's one of the reasons why I wanted to play Dr Cameron, because of Scotland and the time I was young in Scotland. I think he is everybody's image of the old-fashioned GP.

He also delivered many memorable lines in the series, but the one he liked best occurred in a dramatic story about a dead man whose alcoholic old widow would not hand over the body, believing – until the gin ran out – that he was still alive. Andrew's response as Dr Cameron was pungent and full of his own philosophy: 'There is nothing in the human predicament that we cannot laugh at if we hope to survive.'

Andrew had no idea, of course, how successful the series would become. Nor that the press would soon start writing that he had 'raised the character to the level of a national hero', creating 'The Cult of Dr Cameron', as Julian Critchley wrote in *The Times* of 22 February 1969. 'If doctors in this age of factory medicine still come high on our estimation, it is in part due to Dr Cameron,' he claimed, and then went on:

> *Something of a cult of Cameron has grown up among doctors. He belongs to a pre-Fleming era of medicine, to the time before penicillin, when doctors actually saw their patients die. His bedside manner is to be copied if his techniques are not.*

Andrew was intensely conscious of his responsibilities towards the role, both on screen and off, and once turned down a fee of £200,000 to appear in a TV advert for whisky, declaring: 'People would think it was Dr Cameron recommending the product.' He was, though, very fond of a tot or two himself and in 1987 relented on his earlier decision and provided the voice-over for a video, 'Don't Lose Heart', launched by the Chest Heart and Stroke Association, which advised people recovering from heart attacks not to wrap themselves in cotton wool and that alcohol in moderation could be helpful and relaxing. Andrew's part in the campaign earned him the headline in the *Daily Telegraph* of February 1987: 'Ale and hearty, video-cartoon advice from Dr Cameron'.

He was, though, deeply embarrassed by one *faux pas* which he committed in the part. As a man who read poetry, theology and philosophy and could discourse on the finer points of Kierkegaard, Einstein and Wittgenstein, he was horrified to receive a letter from one viewer after he had quoted a line by Gerald Manley Hopkins, 'Glory be to God for dappled things'. The poem had not yet been published at the time Cameron was practising, the correspondent sniffed.

He was very much influential in creating the close rapport with Barbara Mullen and Bill Simpson which undoubtedly gave the series its special flavour, and like the young GP, found the role following him even after the series had long finished. On a visit to Southampton University in 1975, for instance, he was amused when a student called out to him as they passed in the grounds, 'Dr Cameron, where's Janet?'

'If you are exposed for all those years on a Sunday night to an audience of ten to fourteen million, what can you expect?' he asked me. 'In fact, I still get letters from people. Fortunately, not from people wanting to discuss their aches and pains. They just want an autograph or photograph, which is quite amazing.'

'I'm a very lucky man,' I recall his last words to me. 'I've had a tremendously happy life, full of adventure. I shall be quite satisfied if the only part I am remembered for is Dr Cameron.' Andrew died on 29 April 1988.

ON CALL WITH DOCTOR FINLAY

Ian Bannen rolls up his sleeves for an outdoor scene.

a difficult time while Finlay was away at the war, and was looking forward to his retirement. Then he wasn't so sure. For although Finlay is more mature, Cameron still feels the need to keep an eye on him. I have to be a dispenser of whisky and wisdom.

'The storylines are also much more realistic compared to the old series. *Dr Finlay's Casebook* tended to exist in a time warp with a lot of funny jokes about aspirins and things. This series is aimed very much at the 1990s and although there is some strong stuff in the scripts, there is humour, too.

Like his co-stars, Ian has formed a good rapport with the whole production team and says that he is happy to continue playing Cameron, 'as long as the audience enjoys it'. Already there is strong evidence of how the success of *Doctor Finlay* is spreading, even abroad, as Ian can vouch from an experience of his own during a break from filming in 1993.

'My wife Marilyn and I were visiting Prague and decided to go to a performance of *Don Giovanni* at the opera,' he recalled. 'The place was packed, but we managed to get a seat almost at the back. When we came out afterwards, it was dark and there were crowds milling everywhere. Suddenly, this very strong German accent bellowed out behind us: "Ah, Dr Cameron, are you shooting *Doctor Finlay* here in Prague?" Well, naturally, I turned round and said, "No, why do you ask?" The

Andrew when I'm playing Cameron, though,' he went on. 'I've never had this difficulty before, except perhaps when playing Hamlet. You tend to hear other people who have played a part, and in nearly every line, I can hear in the back of my mind the way Andrew would have said it. And I can see that terrible, turned-down mouth he had. Consciously, or sub-consciously, I found myself imitating him while trying damn hard not to. Annette Crosbie told me she found the same thing when she was answering the telephone and saying 'Arden House' in just the same way that Barbara Mullen used to answer it.

'But I think the relationship between the main characters is the most important thing about this series. Cameron certainly had man said: "Well, I have been sitting behind the front row of the stalls and there is Dr Neil with the most beautiful girl and a bottle of champagne, and I wondered!" Marilyn and I were very surprised; and it turned out that Jason was working in Prague on a movie and was just having a night out!'

Although Ian and Marilyn live for much of the time in Phoenix, Arizona, they also have homes in London and on the Isle of Wight. But for Ian there are few greater pleasures than a return trip to Scotland. 'The people are so much friendlier,' he said to me, as our conversation drew to a close. 'In southern England you smile at somebody in the street and they think there's something wrong with you.'

Even more enjoyable for 'the boy from the Brig' as locals in Coatbridge call him, have been his two return visits to his home town while filming *Doctor Finlay*. In 1992, for the third episode of the first series, 'Winning the Peace', he was there for the filming of a war memorial service at Old Monkland Parish Church on Woodside. Then in August 1993, he returned to exactly the same location with the production crew, his three co-stars and eighty extras to film Janet and Angus's wedding day. Here, not that far from 'Bannen's Land', Ian played one of the most significant scenes in the *Finlay* legend. It was an emotional moment for him: as a man, to be performing before the cameras in the location where he had grown up, and as Dr Cameron, about to give away the woman who had been

such a central part of his life for so many years.

'Och, I'm a-thinking,' he said to me as he rose to leave, his voice a soft rumble in his throat, 'that Dr Cameron is maybe regretting he didn't ask Janet to marry *him*!'

And with that, the old raconteur gave me a wink and went out to help continue the legend that he might so easily have started thirty years ago.

Dr Cameron watches with mixed feelings as Janet leaves Arden House with Angus Livingstone.

Doctor Finlay:
Episode Guide

Executive Producer: **Robert Love**

Producer: **Peter Wolfes**

Production Designer: **Marius Van Der Werff**

Directors: **Patrick Lau, Aisling Walsh and
Sarah Pia Anderson**

Script Executive: **Pamela Wilson**

Music: **Richard Harvey**

Series One

(FIRST SHOWN 5 MARCH – 9 APRIL 1993)

Episode 1:
'THE RETURN' by Bill Craig

It is 1946, Berlin. Dr Finlay has completed his last operation before he is to be demobbed, back in Britain. In the small Scottish town of Tannochbrae, Janet MacPherson, the house-keeper, is busily organizing a welcome-home party for him, while Dr Cameron continues to run the Arden House practice single-handed. He is longing to retire to the country cottage he has just bought with the help of a large bank loan.

District Nurse Brenda Maitland is meanwhile anxious at the prospect of John Finlay's return. How is she going to tell her fiancée that she is going to marry another man, an American airman, Sgt Steve Fullarton? She is so worried that she cannot face going to the party at Arden House.

Dr Finlay arrives back to a warm wel-come, marred only by his discovery that the opinionated young man who has pinched his seat on the train and with whom he had been forced to share a taxi from the station, is Dr

Finlay completes his last day at the military hospital in Berlin.

Finlay that she is marrying Steve Fullarton, not him, and he returns dejected to Arden House, only to find that Dr Cameron has engaged Dr Neil as practice locum, without consulting his partner. Cameron is still busy treating patients, although in the case of Agnes Miller – a woman in her thirties with a heart condition – with little success.

Finlay and Neil settle into a war of attrition. Cameron shows Finlay his cottage and reminds him that he wants to retire there soon. As Finlay cannot get a loan from Muir, or any other bank he has tried, the problem seems insoluble. Dr Neil sees his chance and, with his father's financial backing, offers to buy Dr Cameron out. Dr Finlay rejects this out of hand. However, after Neil is called out to see Mrs Miller during Cameron's visit to Ian Granville, an old consultant colleague in Glasgow, Dr Finlay is forced to reconsider Neil's partnership offer.

It seems that Dr Cameron has prescribed for Mrs Miller's heart condition in a dangerous and unethical way, having failed to realize that the woman is pregnant. To protect both his patients and his reputation, the only solution Finlay can see is for him to retire forthwith.

Finlay eventually accepts Neil's offer and confronts Dr Cameron, who agrees to go. Only some days later does the old doctor confess that he was fully aware of Mrs

David Neil, and is to be interviewed by Dr Cameron for the job of locum. Dr Neil does not get a glowing reference from Dr Finlay, who is left reeling by the other news from Dr Cameron that Janet may marry the local chemist, Angus Livingstone.

At the party that evening, there is a frank exchange of views on the proposed National Health Service. Dr Finlay manages to alienate both Dr Gilmore, the influential county Medical Officer of Health, and Mr Muir, the local bank manager. (Mrs Muir has recently become an ex-patient of Dr Cameron since he told her she was 'as healthy as a cow'.) The prospects for Dr Finlay negotiating a bank loan to buy out Dr Cameron's share of the practice are not promising.

Brenda breaks the bad news to Dr

Miller's condition: her case is more complex and confidential than it appeared. Her heart condition meant that her pregnancy was potentially life-threatening, but to the Millers, who are Catholics, abortion is a mortal sin. Nevertheless, Mrs Miller decided to shoulder the burden of that sin alone and Dr Cameron allowed her to do so, with his colleague Ian Grenville's help. He had allowed the two younger doctors to think he was incompetent so that Finlay would accept Neil's partnership offer. Dr Finlay has been out-manoeuvred.

EPISODE 2:
'WORKING TOGETHER'

BY ANN MARIE DI MAMBRO

Now that Dr Finlay and Dr Neil are partners, Dr Cameron is free to leave Arden House. Even though Janet and the two younger doctors are patient and sympathetic towards him, he feels, somewhat irrationally, that he is being forced out. He also believes, this time with good reason, that his successors have failed to form a viable working relationship.

Meanwhile, Dr Gilmore is giving five-star private medical attention to the Findlater family. Mrs Findlater is about to give birth to her longed-for second child. Her eight-year-old daughter, Evelyne, seems insecure about the impending birth, while Mr Findlater, a wealthy local businessman, is delighted when his wife produces a son who can take over the family firm. Much to her mother's concern, Evelyne has watched her in labour, from a vantage point in their hallway. In contrast, Mr Baillie, who works in Findlater's iron foundry,

Dr Neil finally settles in at Arden House as Dr Finlay's new partner in the practice.

is waiting anxiously in his small terraced house, watched by his four children, while his wife Pauline suffers a difficult labour. Despite the combined efforts of Nurse Brenda Maitland and Dr Finlay, her baby is stillborn.

The Grieves family, who run the local greengrocers, are also having problems. Teenage son, Ronnie, who works in the shop is horrified when he inadvertently finds out that his mother, Alison, is giving away her absent husband's clothes. The boy returns them all to his parents' wardrobe which shocks and depresses his mother when she catches sight of them.

Dr Neil has restored Jamie Thomson's sexual potency by a simple procedure, thus earning the young man's undying gratitude in the shape of regular deliveries of poached game. Dr Gilmore, however, is furious with Neil for attending to his private patient Evelyne Findlater, at the request of the young girl's grandmother, Mrs McKinney. She's concerned that her granddaughter is genuinely ill and not merely piqued at the arrival of her baby brother, as Dr Gilmore has suggested. After Evelyne loses control of the baby's pram during a somewhat fraught family picnic, Mr Findlater is convinced that Dr Gilmore's diagnosis is correct.

Dr Finlay attends Ronnie in the shop after he falls off a ladder into some glass display shelves. While treating the boy, the doctor cuts his own hand badly on a hidden shard of glass. He later learns that Ronnie's father is an army commando who has been 'missing in action' for four years. Alison believes her husband is dead but Ronnie is convinced he is alive and has developed an unhealthy obsession with the war.

Finlay is furious to get a call asking him to join Dr Neil at the Findlaters since Neil has obviously ignored Dr Gilmore's justified threats to report him. However, when he gets to the house, he finds Evelyne in a very serious condition. Dr Gilmore cannot be contacted. Neil is stuck for a diagnosis but Finlay realizes just in time what the problem is: fluid has to be drained from around the child's heart, which Finlay's bandaged fingers unfortunately prevent him from doing. He guides Neil through the tricky procedure and between them, they save the child's life.

Back at Arden House, Dr Cameron listens to their tale of the evening's events and realizes it is time for him to leave the two younger men to work together. He goes into the surgery to clear his desk for the last time and then bequeaths it to Dr Finlay with his blessing.

EPISODE 3
'WINNING THE PEACE'

BY MICHAEL WILCOX

Dr Cameron has moved to his country cottage, although Janet is still providing occasional meals at Arden House. He has been co-opted on to the assessment panel at the local German prisoner-of-war camp so, much to his relief, he is still busy. During a visit to check on two German POWs who are working on a remote farm as labourers, he promises to send Dr Finlay to attend to the farmer's wife, Mrs Henderson, who has had a bad fall.

Dr Finlay returns from his farm visit puzzled. Mrs Henderson seemed in good health to him. Janet wonders if the real problem might have been Archie Henderson, the only son, who deserted from the army two years ago and, according to local rumour, is hiding out there. Dr Cameron offers to have another discreet word with the Hendersons.

Cameron arrives in the middle of an army raid instigated by Sergeant Forbes, the local policeman. Forbes' own son was in Archie's regiment but was killed in Sicily and now, bitter for revenge, he has been watching the farm obsessively, hoping to flush Archie out. When the soldiers fail to find Archie and leave empty-handed, Forbes vows to return. The Hendersons then confess to Dr Cameron that they are sheltering Archie and that he needs medical help.

Meanwhile, in Tannochbrae, Reverend Gill is finalizing arrangements for the church memorial service where the Roll of Honour, with all the names of the town's war-dead, will be unveiled. This faces Alison Grieves, the local greengrocer, with a terrible choice. Her husband has been missing in action for four years. Should she have his name included or not? Her son Ronnie, horrified that she is even prepared to consider it, remains convinced that his father is still alive somewhere.

Dr Neil is trying to track down a new drug – Penicillin G – that is hard to come by, for his patient, young Sam Colquhoun. Sam lost a leg at the end of the war, and has also managed to contract a case of syphilis after a night out on the town with his mates. Nurse Brenda Maitland has been dressing Sam's war wound but, too embarrassed, he has not told her about his more delicate problem. She is much amused when Dr Neil reveals all, along with the news that Reverend Gill has invited Neil to join the church choir, where Brenda sings a fine soprano. Dr Neil finds the penicillin Sam needs, much to Dr Gilmore's disgust. He is outraged that young men of dubious morals are being treated with a scarce and expensive drug.

Brenda is told by Steve Fullarton, the American airforce sergeant, that he is being sent home but he has managed to get a passage on a ship for her, from Liverpool to New York. They can soon be married in the States. This news throws Brenda into turmoil and she ends up discussing her misgivings with Janet despite an initial frosty reception from the housekeeper at Arden House.

Dr Finlay examines a truculent and defensive Archie Henderson in his hide-out in the woods. He persuades Archie that the cottage hospital is the best place for his cracked ribs to be tended. Sergeant Forbes is still watching the farm, however, and when they leave with Dr Cameron, he tries to head them off on his bicycle, causing an accident which precipitates a crisis in Archie's breathing. Dr Finlay deals with it promptly and efficiently by inserting a cannula into Archie's lung cavity.

On their way back from settling Archie into hospital, the two doctors are again inter-cepted, this time by a deliriously happy Ronnie Grieves. Colonel Groves Hill, his father's CO, has arrived with the news that his father has been found alive and well in Odessa. He is coming home soon.

On the day of the commemoration service, Dr Neil is suffering from an attack of nerves about his choral début but the service and the singing prove very moving, with Reverend Gill using the occasion to try to restore peace to the troubled community of Tannochbrae.

EPISODE 4:
'A BITTER PILL'

BY JAMES MAVOR

An urgent smallpox vaccination programme is underway in Tannochbrae. In the Salvation Army hall, Dr Gilmore, Dr Finlay, Dr Cameron and District Nurse Brenda Maitland prepare to deal with a hoard of schoolchildren. After taking surgery at Arden House, Dr Neil sets off on a home visit. Railwayman Alan Thomson has asked him to visit his chronically-sick wife, Mary. It is clear that there are tensions between Alan and Mary's father, Jack, who owns the house they all share. Neil examines Mary and notices that she has pills for anaemia which Dr Cameron has prescribed.

One morning when Alan Thomson returns from his night shift at the signal-box, Mary is waiting for him, all dressed up and ready to go shopping. Tired though Alan is, he is delighted to see his wife in such rare good humour. He gives her the iron pills but unknown to him, she does not swallow them. Their outing is then cut short when they encounter Miss Prentice, a former teaching colleague of Mary's whom she clearly does not want to face.

Inside the hall, Janet is tactfully ushering Dr Gilmore out, as Steve arrives to apologize to Brenda for his outburst the previous day when Brenda had told him that she would not be able to see him off to America. To Brenda's discomfort, Steve and Dr Finlay meet for the first time.

Dr Neil seeks Dr Cameron's opinion on Mary Thomson but is not convinced by the older doctor's belief that the patient is not ill

In the Salvation Army hall, Dr Finlay and Nurse Brenda Maitland get the urgent vaccination programme underway.

but unhappy. At the Thomsons' Neil takes a blood sample from Mary. He is bemused by her manner which is both paranoid and flirtatious. After the doctor leaves, Mary viciously rejects Alan's affectionate sympathy, tearing her new nightdress in the process. Later, she allows her father to think that Alan tried to force his attentions on her, as she lay ill in bed. Jack storms out and attacks Alan in the signalbox, all his hatred for him spilling out: his son-in-law is not a 'proper' man. Alan chokes out that he and Mary got married because she was pregnant. Jack refuses to believe it.

The next morning at Arden House, as Janet and Angus Livingstone start to move the last of Dr Cameron's possessions to his new cottage, Dr Neil dresses Alan Thomson's wounds. Alan says he fell but only came to see Neil for the results of Mary's tests. Gently, Neil suggests that his wife may not be taking the pills that were prescribed. Afterwards, in the car with Angus, who is delighted that they can now have more time together, Janet worries that Dr Cameron looked very sad when they left. In fact, the old boy is dancing a jig to the record he is playing on his beloved gramophone.

Alan is determined to make Mary talk to him about the dreadful state of their marriage. Once again, she totally rejects him and Alan walks out. When Dr Neil calls to see Alan, Jack (who has been drinking heavily) refuses to let him in. Later, Jack eats his supper with Mary, as if Alan did not exist.

Dr Finlay has been in surgery, dealing with allergic reactions to the vaccinations, when Brenda arrives to tell him that she wants to withdraw her resignation: she is not going to America to join Steve. Finlay is bemused.

Dawn is breaking. Mary comes downstairs to be greeted by a ghastly sight. Alan has hanged himself. Jack tries to comfort his hysterical daughter. Finlay and Neil arrive just before the police but Alan is already dead. Finlay tries to comfort Neil but the younger doctor is too shocked to respond and walks home alone in the cold morning light, as the ambulance carrying Alan's body drives past him.

EPISODE 5:

'FORBIDDEN FRUIT'

BY COLIN MACDONALD

Anne Stewart, a patient of Dr Finlay's breaks down in the surgery when he implies that her ailments are psychosomatic. Rather abashed and moved by her distress, the doctor comforts her, though he later rebuffs Dr Neil sharply for making a joke about Mrs Stewart 'swooning in his arms'. When Anne admits to Finlay that her real problem is being trapped in a small house, with a husband she cannot confide in, Finlay invites her to come to the new Mothers' Group that he has set up with the Minister's help.

Meanwhile, Dr Cameron is in his element lecturing to German prisoners of war at the local camp, though when he asks Gerd Rentz, the most fluent and friendly of them, to translate an Armistice Day poem into German for him, the man refuses and clams up. Instead of Dr Cameron's usual class, the POW are being shown a film of the German concentration camps. Gerd Rentz barely controls his horrified reaction but when the film ends, he encourages the other men to join him in applauding the Hollywood propaganda. Major Patterson, the camp commander, is incensed by what he sees as a totally callous reaction.

Anne Stewart arrives late at the inaugural meeting of the Mothers' Group, with her children. Dr Finlay watches her, fascinated, as she literally lets her hair down. In church the next day, as Tom Stewart reads the lesson, Janet notices the eye contact between Finlay and Anne and disapproves.

After church, despite Janet's spirited protestations, Angus sweeps her off to lunch at the local hotel and invites her to join him in Glasgow for a weekend. Dr Cameron has just finished his class at the camp and is concerned that Gerd has not turned up. Major Patterson explains Rentz's reaction to the film, declaring that such behaviour is typical of a U-boat man. Dr

Finlay finds his professional position compromised when he becomes attracted to one of his patients, Anne Stewart.

Cameron tries to talk to Gerd who first ignores him, then accuses him of hypocrisy and finally breaks down in despair about the utter inhumanity of the concentration camps he saw in the film. Cameron tries to make him understand that he is not being blamed and that he must go home to his family in Germany and work to rebuild his country.

Finlay drives Anne off into the countryside where despite their intimate talking, he pulls back from the physical contact he longs for, pointing out that she is his patient. When he gets back, both Dr Gilmore and Dr Neil get the sharp end of his tongue, as his guilty conscience reasserts itself. Janet suspects, and is so concerned about him that she visits Dr Cameron to confide her fears.

Tom Stewart has heard about Dr Finlay's visits from customers at his butcher's shop and turns up at surgery and questions a very startled Finlay. Tom tells him he has no alternative but to take his family out of the practice. Finlay goes straight to Anne at the Mothers' Group to tell her that she is no longer his patient. In the church hall kitchen, they kiss passionately but they are interrupted by Anne's friend Mary Gunn who is well aware of what is going on.

When Finlay gets back to Arden House, Dr Cameron is waiting for him and outlines the ethical dilemma of the relationship graphically. The next day, Finlay goes off with Anne when he should be speaking at a meeting organized by Dr Gilmore on the proposed new NHS. Janet sends Dr Neil off to cover for his senior partner: the result is something of a shambles, though Neil thinks he handled it rather well. Finlay tells Anne that if he is to be a doctor they cannot be together.

As normal life goes on in Tannochbrae, Anne Stewart takes her children and a few possessions to the outskirts of the town and leaves on a bus bound for Edinburgh. Finlay is grieving at the same spot where he walked with her the day before, as Janet waits and worries at Arden House and a desolate Tom Stewart reads the farewell note his wife has left for him.

To Janet's relief, Finlay finally returns to Arden House. The next day, he visits a patient who is something of a local Mrs Malaprop. There he finds to his surprise that he can still laugh: the doctor's life, too, goes on.

EPISODE 6:
'THE GOOD DOCTOR'

BY JAMES MAVOR

As Janet has gone off to Glasgow with the chemist, Angus Livingstone, Dr Neil is cooking, or rather burning breakfast. He offers to do the rounds and leaves a taciturn Finlay to take surgery but when Neil sees the famous singer Margaret Williams in the waiting room, he changes his mind. She reveals to the starstruck young doctor that she is staying at Forrigan, with Lord and Lady Mackenzie and has called in with a letter from her doctor in Harley Street, authorizing a repeat prescription for painkillers.

Dr Finlay's first call of the day is at the Forrigan estate lodge where he examines the gamekeeper, Archie Reid. Finlay prescribes rest for the man's bad leg, advice Archie cannot take if the is to continue to do his job properly. On his way back through Tannochbrae, Finlay encounters Dr Gilmore and the two men cross swords again about the NHS. The dispute is halted when a resentful Finlay has to move his car to allow the Mackenzies to pass in their chauffeur-driven saloon. Back at Arden House, Janet has returned from Glasgow and is dispensing sherry and Battenberg cake. Finlay is less than pleased to be reminded by Dr Neil that Roddy, a varsity chum of his, is coming for the weekend.

The two doctors are grappling with a recalcitrant young patient, Tommy Collins, as Dr Cameron chats to Janet in the kitchen. Dr Neil boasts about his encounter with Margaret Williams but the wind is taken out of his sails when Cameron announces that he is off to lunch with the Mackenzies today. As he stops in town, Neil's friend Roddy Forsyth roars into town on his motorbike.

At Forrigan, Cameron puts his foot in it when he reveals in front of his hosts that Margaret called in to the surgery at Arden House, although Margaret glosses over the moment with great social ease.

Neil introduces Brenda to Roddy after choir practice. She treats his efforts to flirt with her with amused tolerance. Finlay is dining with Dr Cameron at his cottage but the atmosphere becomes tense when his host refers to Anne Stewart, as an ex-patient that Finlay fell in love with. Finlay still blames his old partner for interfering and tells him that he has been invited to join a friend who has set up a new practice in Canada.

Their evening is interrupted when Cameron is urgently summoned to Forrigan to see Margaret, who has been taken ill. She confesses her sad secret to him: she has terminal cancer. Cameron reassures Lord and Lady Mackenzie about their guest but remains the soul of discretion and is very moved by the situation. Meanwhile, the Forrigan shoot is in process. Archie is finding the going hard, with his bad leg. Gilmore is in his element, having narrowly escaped being mown down on his way to the shoot by the motorbike hellraisers Roddy Forsyth and David Neil.

Sunday lunch is underway at Arden House, with Janet, Angus, Roddy, Neil and Finlay. The atmosphere is somewhat strained. Finlay finds Roddy hard to stomach and the lad's assumption that Janet is Angus's wife is nearly the last straw. However, it does encourage Angus to tell Janet that she must finally decide whether she is going to accept his proposal of marriage or not.

Finlay calls in to the Reids again. Brenda is there, showing Archie some exercises for his leg. As Finlay explains to Archie's wife, Betty, that her husband will have to have an operation and is unlikely to be able to continue as a gamekeeper afterwards. Finlay fumes to Brenda about the Mackenzies' exploitation of their workers. Brenda has a more balanced view and points out to Finlay that his own need to work is just as great as Archie's; the class divide is not the relevant issue. Late that night, Finlay is in the surgery, filling in an application form to practice medicine in Canada.

When he comes down to breakfast the next morning, the table is bare and he finds a very upset Janet in the kitchen. She is in turmoil about Angus's proposal. Finlay learns that Archie will have to wait a long time for the operation he needs on his leg and sets off for Forrigan to ask Lord Mackenzie if he will pay for it to be done privately. To his great surprise, the answer is 'yes' and is followed by an invitation to luncheon, where Finlay is as charmed by Margaret as his colleagues have been, though he confesses to her that he has never heard her sing.

Most of Tannochbrae has been invited to the recital that Margaret is giving at Forrigan. Dr Neil is the first to learn that Janet and Angus are engaged to be married; and Dr Finlay mends his fences with Cameron when he tells him he has decided against Canada. He is staying. Margaret Williams' exquisite voice soars through the grand old house.

SERIES TWO

(FIRST SHOWN 18 MARCH – 22 APRIL 1994)

EPISODE 1:

'A DELICATE BALANCE'

BY JAMES MAVOR

Annie, an old friend of Dr Neil's, has come to stay and everyone but he anticipates romance. A mains pipe has burst in Tannochbrae causing flooding in Arden House. Everyone mucks in to make morning surgery more bearable.

Tom Cairns, a local shepherd, startles John Moore as he bathes under a waterfall. John falls, injuring his leg. When Dr Finlay and Brenda arrive, John Moore says that his father is dead. At the Moore's bothy, they find that William Moore is not dead but unconscious and in need of urgent medical attention. At the cottage hospital, Finlay and Gilmore discover that William Moore has terminal stomach cancer.

Back at Arden House, an under-motivated Dr Neil examines four year-old Robbie Hamilton. The boy has been listless and poorly. Neil assures Mrs Hamilton that there is nothing wrong with her son that fresh air and fresh vegetables won't cure. She is unconvinced and when she meets Dr Cameron in the street, she asks him to look at her son. Cameron explains that he has retired but he spots that Robbie has a stiff neck. When he arrives at Arden House for a dinner to celebrate Janet and Angus Livingstone's engagement, he suggests to Neil that he takes a second look at the boy.

Dr Neil finds that Robbie Hamilton has the symptoms of tuberculous meningitis. Mrs Hamilton wants to know why yesterday Neil said that Robbie was run down and today he's saying that her son is going to die.

Cairns tells Dr Finlay that John Moore has discharged himself. He also mentions that the father, William Moore, was a tyrant who practically held his son a prisoner. Finlay re-examines William Moore and finds that the skin on his feet and his hands have hardened, (a condition known as hyperkeratosis). Later, he sees John Moore limping along the road and stops to speak to him. John is very defensive and explains that he cannot go back to the hospital to watch his father die all over again.

Dr Neil reports back to Cameron on Robbie's condition. Cameron is disturbed to hear that Neil has worried Mrs Hamilton with the news that it may be TBM before any tests have been done. Cameron offers to take Mrs Hamilton to the hospital for the tests, but Neil insists that he go too.

Dr Neil explains to Finlay how bad he feels about his mis-diagnosis of Robbie. Later, he pours his feelings out to Annie who tries to convince him that he is a good doctor. Finlay and Neil attend the death of William Moore. They puzzle over the causes of hyperkeratosis – one of which is poisoning. John Moore is in the bothy. He searches the room and finds a pile of banknotes under the mattress, but he is unable to touch the money.

The following morning, Cameron arrives at Arden House with Robbie and Mrs Hamilton in his car. He has difficult news for Neil. Mrs Hamilton doesn't want Neil to come with them. Finlay asks Neil to guard the fort as he has to check up on something. Neil warns Finlay that the Moore case is no longer

A concerned Janet returns Rachel Gant to Oakvale House after the death of Rachel's mother.

Finlay's responsibility. It should be in the hands of the police by now, but Finlay wants to do things his own way. Meanwhile, Cameron tries to comfort Mrs Hamilton as Robbie undergoes a lumbar puncture. The results will be telephoned through to Arden House that same day.

Dr Finlay visits John Moore at the bothy and tells him that his father is dead. John tells Finlay how he wanted to escape his father but could not bring himself to go. When John realizes that Finlay has put two and two together, he confesses that he poisoned his father with sheep dip. Finlay points out that his father did not die from poisoning but from a gastric carcinoma. The final irony is that his father would have died anyway. The huge act of will it took to poison him now counts for nothing. Distressed by his own failure, John is frightened when Cairns' bearded face appears at the window. John runs out pursued by Finlay. John stumbles and falls into the gulley taking Finlay with him.

Dr Neil rushes to the telephone expecting to hear the results of Robbie Hamilton's tests but the call is from the police reporting Finlay's accident. When the phone rings again, Neil's apprehension returns. Dr Neil faces the unenviable task of informing Mrs Hamilton that Robbie does in fact have TBM. Back at the cottage hospital, Dr Neil sits beside an embarrassed Dr Finlay as he lies strapped up in bed. The pair of them admit to each other that they've made a mess of things.

EPISODE 2:
'CHILDSPLAY'

BY PETER J HAMMOND

Dr Finlay watches as thirteen year-old Hannah Berry marches her two young sisters into the surgery. Although it is Sarah who has a slight cold, it is the healthy Hannah who worries Finlay with an adult demeanour far beyond her years.

Dr Neil visits Robbie Hamilton at the Levenvale TB hospital but Dr Reid is annoyed to see him there. Surely, Dr Neil has patients back in Tannochbrae to concern himself with? When Dr Neil asks if Robbie can be given a course of Streptomycin, Dr Reid points out that the new drug is not only scarce, but is still undergoing trials. Dr Neil could spend his time more wisely listening to Mrs Hamilton's wishes and stay away from her son.

Dr Cameron brings Finlay a hand-delivered letter from the builder. When Finlay is shocked to see an outrageous quotation of £534, Cameron hopes that this will put paid to Finlay's grandiose schemes once and for all. Janet has alternative plans.

Dr Finlay's curiosity leads him to Hannah Berry's house with Brenda who tells him that the authorities have been notified because Hannah has been avoiding school to look after her sisters. Her mother went to work at Bright's factory when her husband left to find work in London. Finlay expresses his concern for Hannah and Brenda points out that, although Hannah may need help, she may not know how to ask for it. Later, when Finlay approaches Hannah, however, she explains to him that her mother works full-time and gets very tired.

When Mrs Berry arrives home and opens a letter from her husband, the children learn that their father's job in Kent has fallen through. Hannah is upset to see that, again, her father has sent no money. Hannah hears her mother's body thrashing about on the bedroom floor. Her sisters are terrified but she leaps into action, grabbing the smelling salts and rushing upstairs.

Meanwhile, Cameron sees Janet's advertisement for a housekeeper in the newsagent's window and it seems that feelings for Janet run deeper than he realizes. Dr Neil confesses to Cameron that he has seen Robbie Hamilton and is hopeful for his survival. Cameron states that Neil's hope is misguided. Nevertheless, Neil intends to see Professor Chalmers, the head of the Streptomycin trials in Glasgow. Finlay is pleased when Janet shows him how, with a few sums, Dr Finlay can reduce the cost of his renovations from £534 to a mere £53, although the

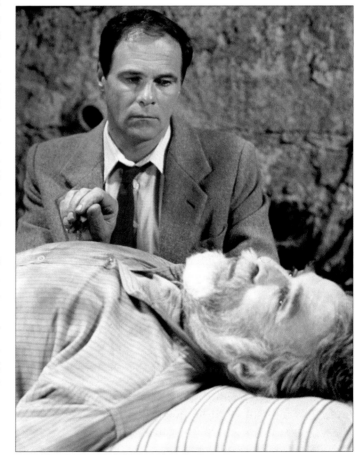

Dr Finlay examines William Moore and makes a startling discovery.

cosmetic job that Janet has in mind is not quite what he had planned.

When the school-attendance officer pays a visit to the Berrys, Hannah hides her sisters. The frustrated officer is unable to persuade them to open the door and marches off to the factory to see Mrs Berry herself. Mrs Berry watches in fear as the school-attendance officer approaches her from one direction and Brenda approaches from another. She leaves her work at the loom and disappears into a locker room, only to fall, her body thrashing around on the floor. Cameron arrives and says that Mrs Berry appears to have had an epileptic fit. He sends her to the cottage hospital.

Dr Neil manages to get past Professor Chalmers' assistant and doorsteps the man himself. Chalmers points out that a course of Streptomycin can last for up to one hundred days and the chances for Robbie at this stage are remote. He does, however, agree to see the boy at Levenvale Hospital

Finlay is shocked to hear that Mrs Berry may have epilepsy and is determined that the Berry children can no longer be left on their own, he visits Hannah to tell her what has happened. Hannah insists that she can still look after her mother but when Finlay has to shout at her to stop and listen, Hannah wets herself and rushes off upstairs. Dr Finlay then finds out from her sister where their Auntie Sheila lives.

Chalmers tells Dr Neil that Robbie is too far gone to benefit from Streptomycin. Neil feels that had he not missed the boy's condition on first examination, he might have saved him. Professor Chalmers stresses that it would not have made any difference because of the scarcity of the drug and asks Dr Neil if he is really cut out to work as a family doctor. Maybe he should take a leaf out of his friend Dr Cameron's book and learn to distance himself. Neil is shocked to learn that Cameron

knows Professor Chalmers and indeed must have told Chalmers to see him.

Hannah and her sisters walk down the street again. This time Hannah is in uniform. She is going back to school.

EPISODE 3:
'STOLEN LIVES'

BY SIMON DONALD, FROM A STORY BY MICHAEL WILCOX

Alec Gant' gasps his last breath as his wife Izabel watches him, attended by Dr Neil and a group of devout church elders. Izabel is choked, not with grief but rage. With Alec's death came the revelation that her daughter Rachel had been detained in an asylum for the last thirty-eight years at Alec Gant's request.

In the Oakvale House asylum, Rachel Gant and her friend Lillian are washing the corpse of a dead woman, one of the many tasks staff are happy to have the more *compos mentis* inmates perform.

When Janet finds out that her old school friend Rachel had not run away to have a baby but was incarcerated, she too is incensed. Finlay is also horrified that, with just two medical certificates as a petition, Rachel's father was able to commit his own daughter to an asylum, essentially as punishment for an under-age pregnancy. Finlay is further outraged to see the names of the original medical signatories.

Janet promises Izabel that she and Elspeth Strickland, another old school friend of Rachel's, will do everything they can do to get her released. Elspeth Strickland then discovers that Rachel can be released with just a written request from her mother and the permission of the medical superintendant at the asylum.

Janet finds Burns and Nimmo, two of the church elders, trying to convince Izabel that it is not in the interests of her health to have Rachel back at home. She tells Izabel that the medical superintendant approved Rachel's release and her daughter is free to come home that very afternoon.

When Janet and Elspeth arrive to collect Rachel from Oakvale House, Matron Smedly is surprised to hear of Rachel's father's death but insists that, now Rachel is no longer her responsibility, it is up to Elspeth and Janet to tell her. When Elspeth finally tells her, Rachel wants to know if Elspeth's father Samuel Strickland is dead too.

Rachel arrives home surprised at how little has changed, except her mother. Janet leaves to share her joy at Rachel's release with Angus. Meanwhile, Elspeth Strickland pulls her car over on to the roadside and sobs.

Burns tells Reverend Gill that Elspeth's mother is not dead as the Minister assumed. She ran away and left Samuel and Elspeth to fend for themselves. Izabel finally asks Rachel who was the father of her child. Rachel insists that the baby was born dead and does not, therefore, have a father.

Cameron, already concerned about Rachel's release, takes issue with Finlay's 'holier than thou' attitude over her and explains how Rachel had attacked the father of one of her friends, tearing at him with her nails; she also apparently tried to take her own life when she was eight months pregnant. Dr Nimmo, who organized all the committal papers, informed Cameron that Rachel had subsequently lost her mind and as far as he knew, Rachel was still insane.

Janet takes Rachel shopping but she bolts at the sight of Elspeth Strickland. And her introduction to Angus Livingstone and his newly-arrived young niece Rhona shows how out of kilter she is in the community.

Rachel, Janet, Elspeth Strickland and Maisie Forfar visit the manse as guests of Reverend Gill. They try to welcome her but Rachel resists, reminding Elspeth that one of the schoolboys put his hand down her knickers. Later, Rachel follows Gill into the kitchen and asks why everyone is talking about her. Gill explains that they all want to know about her and they all love her. Misinterpreting this, she tells Gill that he can sleep with her – just as Janet walks into the room. As Janet and Rachel leave, Rachel tells her that she remembers Elspeth's father and how his jaggy beard used to scratch her.

At home Izabel Gant is dying. Rachel finds her on the bedroom floor and hauls her back into bed. As Izabel's life ebbs away, she finally realizes that Samuel Strickland was the father of Rachel's baby. Then she dies and later, downstairs, Rachel washes her mother's body on the kitchen table. Finally Janet and Elspeth drive her back to Oakvale House where she is reunited with a very happy Lillian. As they drive away, Janet realizes that Elspeth has known the truth about Rachel and her father, Samuel Strickland, all along.

EPISODE 4:
'BURNING BRIDGES'

BY ANDY SMITH

Dr Cameron visits his old friend, Professor Chalmers, who tells him that he wants to employ a young doctor by the name of David Neil as a research fellow; although, after the death of Robbie Hamilton, Chalmers does have his reservations about the young doctor's ability to detach himself from his patients. Cameron reassures Chalmers that Dr Neil just needs to work on a broader canvas. Later that day, the telephone rings in Arden House and

Neil rushes to answer it. Professor Chalmers gives Neil until Friday to make a decision. Finlay then arrives and Dr Neil puts the telephone down and leaves the building, complaining about the lack of privacy.

The decorators arrive at Arden House and Janet is shocked to see that the foreman is a Mr Rattery. Rattery seems intent on reminding Janet exactly why she remembers him. Later, Rattery whistles the Charleston to Janet and reminds her of when she was young Miss MacPherson, much to her extreme annoyance.

Neil walks with Rhona, Angus's niece, as they talk about the demise of Robbie Hamilton and Dr Neil's inability to cope with death. Later, Dr Neil spends some time alone by the river before turning back to Arden House, filled with resolve. That same afternoon, Neil calls Professor Chalmers and accepts the research post. Now he can tell Dr Finlay that he is moving on. With his plans for expanding the practice, Finlay does not take the news well, and Dr Neil precipitates an argument by calling Finlay 'a tin god surrounded by peasants'. When Neil reminds Finlay of his losing Brenda to Steve Fullarton, Finlay punches Neil and they fight in amongst the wet paint and decorator's ladders. Later, as they clean and stitch each other's wounds, Dr Neil observes to Finlay that their confrontation was the most alive he has ever seen him.

Janet interviews two women for the post of housekeeper at Arden House before deciding that she would like her job to be passed on to someone much more full of life than the rather staid applicants. She expresses her feelings to Angus as Rhona looks on, her eyes wide with interest.

Dr Gilmore turns his patients away in order to devote himself to trying to stop his wife's drinking; but he is impotent as he watches Madge pour another tumbler of whisky down her throat. When Madge asks him if he ever loved her, Gilmore cannot answer. Later, Madge threatens to go shopping, playing on her husband's fear that she will be seen drunk in public. Gilmore can only hide his face in his hands in an attempt to black it all out. Late at night, Madge appears at the top of the stairs, dressed in her wedding gown, her mascara streaming down her face. Madge becomes delirious as Gilmore attempts to calm her; but his efforts are in vain and, in desperation, he drives to Cameron's cottage to plead for help.

Back at the Gilmore's residence, Dr Cameron sedates Madge and turns his attention to Gilmore, angry at the fact that Gilmore let his wife get to such a level of deterioration before asking for help. Gilmore, however, cares only for his career and his reputation.

Cameron spends the night watching over Madge. In the early hours, she wakes and propositions Cameron, who feels the night has been long enough. Wearily, he telephones Brenda and asks her to relieve him. Brenda arrives and spends time with Madge who tells Brenda how she had died inside trying to be the model doctor's wife, Gilmore sits in another room, alone, and sobs into his wife's wedding gown. He finally faces the reality of Madge's drink problem, and realizes that his career and reputation will have to be sacrificed.

EPISODE 5:
'SECRECY'

BY PETER J HAMMOND

In a farmer's croft high above Tannochbrae, Dr Finlay examines McFarlane's groin and tells Mrs McFarlane that her husband needs an ambulance. Finlay rushes to find the nearest telephone and when he sees a man dressed in a huge brimmed hat walking in a field, he calls out. The man in the hat ignores Finlay and walks into a large, desolate house in the distance. When Finlay returns to Arden House he complains to Cameron about the stranger and his refusal to help in a time of need. But Cameron is busy complaining about Finlay's recent 'improvements' to the decor of Arden House. Janet informs Finlay that the man Finlay saw is James Geddie, a recluse. Finlay returns to Mrs McFarlane with the news that her husband has a strangulated hernia and requires surgery. He also enquires about James Geddie, whom, it turns out, Mrs McFarlane knows, and finds out that the Geddie house is an unhappy one. Finlay goes for another look and again sees the mysterious figure walking across the moor.

Dr Gilmore has decided to retire to look after his wife, Madge. Finlay wants Gilmore's patients to boost his per capita income after the introduction of the NHS. Gilmore has sold his house and is keen to pass on the goodwill (his patients and their records) to Finlay – but at a price of £1,200. This convinces Cameron that Gilmore is merely trying it on and he worries that with Dr Neil leaving, Finlay may be taking on far too many patients. Finlay, however, sees the value of this investment: on the one hand, he knows how badly Gilmore worries about his reputation and needs to escape stories of the doctor with the alcoholic wife; on the other hand, he also appreciates how Gilmore would have been better off had he sold his house and practice as a going concern, rather than merely as a private residence. So Finlay visits Gilmore to talk business on a more reasonable basis. Gilmore eventually agrees to a reduced price.

A youth appears at Angus's store and asks for a cough prescription for James Geddie. Angus is puzzled by the signature on the prescription and looks in his files. The youth returns to the Geddie house, the doors are unbolted one by one, and he is asked inside. Cameron later explains to Finlay that Geddie used to be his patient but ceased to be under him, simply by dint of his protracted absence from Cameron's visiting list. Geddie, apparently, is an obsessive. Angus shows Finlay the signature on the prescription and says that it is not James Geddie's. If the signature is a fake. Finlay wonders, then who lives in the Geddie house?

Angus's niece, Rhona, helps Dr Neil to pack his things and leave a 'tidy ship'. Unfortunately, however, Rhona's help with the patients' records means that what Dr Neil gets is far from tidiness.

Finlay finds out from Mrs McFarlane that she used to work for the Geddie family and that both parents were killed in an hotel fire, in Edinburgh. Some people even reported that James Geddie had a sister who was sent away when she was young. Back on the moor, the mysterious figure bends double coughing. The wind whips the hat away and reveals a mass of long hair and a woman's face. In Arden House, Finlay discovers through Cameron that Geddie became obsessed with the danger of fire after his parents were killed. Finlay rushes back to the Geddie house and is stopped by the youth, who asks Finlay to attend to his sick mother, inside. James Geddie appears and demands to know why Finlay is there; but he is more concerned to know if Finlay has brought any matches with him. Finlay examines Miss Geddie's chest, diagnosing bronchial pneumonia, and Geddie explains that his sister returned to take care of him after many years, having been sent away by their parents for becoming pregnant out of marriage. Although it appears at first that Geddie's sister murdered her parents in revenge, it finally becomes evident to Finlay that the act of arson was not an act of revenge, but a creation of James's obsessive mind.

EPISODE 6:
'IN ARCADIA'

BY ANDY SMITH

When, one morning, Dr Finlay leaves Arden House for his usual rounds he finds an irate Dr Cameron kicking the punctured tyre on his car. Together, they agree to collect the 'bits and pieces' for that night's celebrations. Finlay arrives at a humble croft where the MacIntyre children, Sheila, Edward and Charlie, are all suffering from measles. Mrs Shona MacIntyre tells Finlay that Edward's health is much improved and he is itching to get out of his cramped house. Finlay advises Shona that Edward should remain indoors until he is better.

Esme, Rhona's mother, arrives with Rhona's Aunt Flora, and a wedding dress she made for Janet. Rhona is not happy to see her mother in Tannochbrae but puts on her very best face.

Young Edward MacIntyre cannot ignore his desire to escape the darkened croft and steals out when his mother is busy making soup. Meanwhile, Jamie, a sheep farmer, finds one of his animals dead in the bracken: it has been savaged by a dog. Not far away, Hamish Wilde's horse shies as Hamish loads sheaves of hay on to his cart. Hamish turns and is attacked by a large dog.

Cameron finally manages to find a tyre – at the expense of issuing a sick note to enable its donor to attend Ayr races. Inside Arden House, Janet checks her kitchen ware for the last time and quietly sheds a tear.

Hamish cycles into town, blood streaming from his face, as the whole of rural Tannochbrae takes up arms in search of the dog. He reaches Arden House where Cameron

tries to reassure him that he does not have rabies: there has been no case of indigenous rabies in Scotland since 1903. But Hamish has seen rabid humans in India during the war and is convinced that the dog he saw was rabid. He wants the treatment for rabies, however painful it may be; but Cameron refuses, confident that the chances of Hamish having rabies are non-existent.

Rhona tells her mother that she has absolutely no intention of returning to Edinburgh but plans to stay in Tannochbrae and become the housekeeper at Arden House once Janet is married. Esme is not happy that her daughter is to become a 'skivvy'.

Finlay arrives at Arden House with two cock pheasants which Cameron immediately sets about dressing with his scalpel. On the table sits a feast fit for a queen.

At the MacIntyre croft, Shona MacIntyre finds Edward missing and is torn between searching for him and leaving Sheila and Charlie alone, sick in their beds. Eventually she leaves but becomes hysterical as she searches the moor for Edward. As the hunters' hounds track the scent of the dog, they find Edward, cold and unconscious, but still breathing. Jamie orders some men to take Edward to the cottage hospital; the others he orders to continue their hunt for the dog.

Esme, Rhona and Flora fit Janet's dress and when Janet sees herself in the mirror she is truly amazed. She had never seen herself as a beautiful woman before. Later, she meets Angus on the bridge over the river and asks him for his understanding: unlike Angus,

Janet is inexperienced in marriage.

Cameron invites Esme and Flora to dine with them but Rhona is upset and leaves Arden House to be close to her Uncle Angus on the eve of his marriage. Rhona understands why her father threw Esme out: she is a difficult, greedy and cruel woman who always seems to get what she wants, at everyone else's expense. Angus tells Rhona not to let Esme drive her away from Tannochbrae and advises her to return to the dinner party.

Brenda and Dr Neil arrive and everyone sits down to enjoy the feast that Cameron and Finlay have prepared. Rhona helps Janet to serve and Janet presents her with a compilation of her own recipes gathered over the years

Dr Cameron finally gives Janet away at her wedding to Angus Livingstone.

at Arden House. A truck load of farmers arrives at Arden House and interrupts the proceedings, just as Janet and Cameron are reminiscing to the tune of a piper. The farmers produce the dead dog, and Cameron tells them to take it to the ministry vet so that they can reassure Hamish once and for all that the dog was not rabid. When Finlay and Neil are away, the piper modulates into a lilting dance and Janet and Cameron dance in the moonlight. The following day of the wedding eventually dawns and Cameron leads Janet down the aisle, giving her his blessing as he gives her away to

DOCTOR FINLAY:
CAST LIST

Dr John Finlay ....David Rintoul
Dr Alexander Cameron ....Ian Bannen
Janet MacPherson ....Annette Crosbie
Dr David Neil...............................Jason Flemyng
Angus Livingstone ....Gordon Reid
Brenda Maitland ....Margo Gunn
Dr Gilmore ....Ralph Riach
Madge Gilmore ....Monica Gibb
Reverend Gill.................................... James Telfer
Rhona Swanson...................................... Jackie Morrison

Agnes Miller ....Gerda Stevenson
Alan Thomson ....John McGlynn
Alison Grieves ....Barbara Horne
Anne Stewart.........................Patricia Kerrigan
Annie ....Hilary McLean
Archie Henderson...................Brian McCardie
Archie Reid ....Harry Jones
Baillie Budge...................................John Dair
Betty Reid...................................Sheila Donald
Cheeky boy..................................John Fernon
Col Groves-Hill ....Frank Moorey
Douglas Findlater.....................John McEnery
Dr Granville ....Raymond Ross
Dr Nimmo ....James Maxwell
Dr Reid ....Lawrie McNicol
Elspeth Strickland...............Eileen McCallum
Evelyne Findlater ....Shiona Martin
Frances Findlater..................Lindy Whiteford

Gerald Hynde ....Colin McCredie
Gerd Rentz....................................Wolf Kahler
Hannah Berry ....Gillian Reith
Izabel Gant ....Edith McArthur
Jack Molloy..............................Jack Kavanagh
James Geddie ....Kevin McMonagle
Jamie Thomson ....Martin McCardie
Jean Geddie...............................Sara Stewart
John Moore............................Eoin McCarthy
Lady MacKenzie ....Jennifer Piercey
Lillian..........................Anne Marie Timoney
Lord MacKenzie ....Mark Kingston
Maisie Forfar ....Nancy Mitchell
Major Paterson......................Chris Jenkinson
Margaret Williams ....Alison Fiske
Mrs Monaghan ....Elspeth MacNaughton
Mary Calder..........................Daniela Nardini
Mary Thomson ....Sandy McDade

The cast and crew of Doctor Finlay.

Matron Smedley ....Muriel Romanes
McLennan ....Frank Gallagher
Miriam Berry ....Stephanie Elliot
Miss Walters ....Lynn Christie
Mr Baillie ....Andrew Barr
Mr Burns ....Finlay Welsh
Mr Henderson ....Ken Drury
Mr Miller.....................................Jim Byars
Mr Muir....................................David McKail
Mr Strickland ....Phil McCall
Mrs Baillie ....Sharon Erskine
Mrs Berry....................................Anne Lacey
Mrs Black ....Sheila Latimer
Mrs Hamilton.......................Jannette Foggo
Mrs Henderson......................Eileen Nicholas
Mrs McKinney ....Rowena Cooper
Mrs Muir....................................Pamela Kelly
Nurse Flowers ....Jane Reilly

Patterson.......................................Duncan Bell
PC Stoddart...............................Joe Mullaney
Police Sgt Forbes ....Derek Anders
Professor Chalmers ....Frank Middlemass
Rachel Gant ....Anne Kristen
Rattery ....Joseph Brady
Robbie ....Graeme Sharp
Roddy Forsyth ....George Anton
Ronnie Grieves ....Stephen Craig
Sam Colquhoun ....James Convey
Sarah Berry.....................................Lisa Adam
Sgt Steve Fullarton......................Sam Douglas
Tom Cairns ....Iain Agnew
Tom Stewart ....Stevan Rimkus
(Stunts)......................................Gareth Milne,
................................Tip Tipping, Jim Dowdall

CREW LIST

SERIES I AND II

Executive Producer: Robert Love
Producer: Peter Wolfes
Director: Patrick Lau
Aisling Walsh
Sarah Pia Anderson

Production Manager: Brian Donovan
Production Accountant: Jennifer Booth
Cost Accountant: Naeem Sattar
Script Executive: Pamela Wilson
Researcher: Ken Neil
Mark Grindle
Casting: Anne Henderson
Julia Duff
David Wallace

Location Managers: Brian Kaczynski
Lloret Mackenna
Catherine MacFarlane
Location Assistant: Shirley Sinclair
P.A./Continuity: Sheila Johnston
P.A. (Eps 4/5/6) prep: Lynda McCaig
1st Assistant Director: Alan J. Wands
David Brown
Roy Stevens
2nd Assistant Director: Tommy Gormley
Alison Goring
Karen McConnell
3rd Assistant Director: David Gilchrist
Ben Johnston
Production Secretary: Moira MacKinney
Anne O'Neill
Production Designer: Marius Van Der Werff
Art Director: Zoe Macleod
Ken Wheatley
Design Assistants: Cas Stewart
David Jennings
Katrina Thomson
John Amabile
Andy Stokes
Production Buyers: Alex MacDougall
Sue Morrison
Film Editor: Fergus McKinnon
Chris Buckland
Assistant Editor: Fiona McGregor
Lynn Morrison
Dubbing Editor: Douglas MacDougall
Asst. Dubbing Editor: Micheal MacKinnon
Dubbing Mixer: Cy Jack
Aad Wirtz
Costume Designer: Leigh Bellis
Wardrobe Assistants: Clare Pettifer
Sara Keith

Make-up Designer: Anne Hamilton
Make-up Assistants: Fiona Harvey
Annette Conte
Catherine Shirley
Production Runner: Dennis McDermot
Jonathan Farmer
Stephen Docherty
Director of Photography: Jim Peters
Camera operator: Oliver Cheesman
Alison Chapman
Focus Puller: Lorna Will
Camera Assistant: Alan Maxwell
Alan McSheehy
Sound Recordist: Cameron Crosbie
Brian Milliken
Boom Operator: Rosie Straker
Pete Murphy
Grips: Iain Johnstone
John Dowden
Gaffer Electrician: Ian Campbell
Electricians: Hector Robertson
Robert Allan
David Mair
Frank McConalogue
Stuart Farmer
Robin Johnston
Generator: Brian McGhee
Stage Chargehands: Tony McIlmurray
Jeff Holmes
Dressing Stagehands: Steve Collins
Phil Mann
John Thomson
Props: Ron Nicol
Allan Campbell
Props Store Keeper: Mary Dawson
Construction Manager: Peter Dickson
Painter: Henry Gallagher
Jim O'Donnell
Joiner: Bert Ross
Drivers: John Edwards (Fac)
Arthur Morrison
Caterer: VIP
Wardrobe Bus: Haldane's
Makeup Bus: Cabervans
BFTS

Binkie Darling
Darren Finch
Joanne Slater
Eleanor Baker
Mandy Bryans

— 128 —